Guidance in Esoteric Training

GUIDANCE IN ESOTERIC TRAINING

From the Esoteric School

RUDOLF STEINER

RUDOLF STEINER PRESS
London

Translation revised by C. Davey and O. Barfield, with supplementary material translated by M. Barton, J. Collis, R. Stebbing and M. Cotterell

Rudolf Steiner Press
51 Queen Caroline Street
London W6 9QL

www.rudolfsteinerpress.com

First published (in a shorter version) by Rudolf Steiner Press 1972
Reprinted 1977
Second edition (enlarged) 1994
Third edition 1998, reprinted 2001

This volume contains extracts from the book first published in German under the title *Anweisungen für eine esoterische Schulung*, number 245 in the *Rudolf Steiner Gesamtausgabe* or Collected Works published by Rudolf Steiner Verlag, Dornach. (Volume 245 has now been discontinued and replaced by the fuller publication of esoteric texts in volumes 264–268.) This authorized translation is published by kind permission of the Rudolf Steiner Nachlassverwaltung, Dornach

This edition also includes an extract from lecture XI of *The Human Soul in Relation to World Evolution* (Anthroposophic Press, 1984) and 'Advice on Meditation given by Rudolf Steiner' from *Anthroposophical Movement* (November 1951 and January–April 1952)

Translation © Rudolf Steiner Press 1994

A catalogue record for this book is available from the British Library

ISBN 1 85584 076 6

Cover by Andrew Morgan
Typeset by DP Photosetting, Aylesbury, Bucks.
Printed and bound in Great Britain by Cromwell Press Limited, Trowbridge, Wilts.

Contents

VII

Foreword to the Second Edition

Since the year 1972 when this book was first available in English, the demand for esoteric training has increased to an overwhelming degree. Just at the time of the first printing, a whole generation of younger people world-wide had begun to experience that the mechanistic, utilitarian, materialistic attitude and relationship to life no longer could provide a basis for their own entrance into twentieth-century civilization. They began to search in a far more intensive — sometimes even frantic — way for means towards self-discovery than had been the case for their parents or grandparents, who were absorbed and burdened through war and the immense technological challenges which accompany war and its aftermath. Now, in retrospect, at the end of the century it is apparent that the last third of this century bears witness to countless human beings who know with inner certainty that their own development in the skills of modern life, in social relationships and in spiritual dimensions is not limited in effect to them only but simultaneously affects the earth, the universe and humanity in general. Thus they have become earnest seekers imbued with the will to find various means for self-development.

Rudolf Steiner's life work was devoted to these needs of modern humanity. Today we find the impulses which sprang from his initiatives in numerous fields of endeavour, such as education, medicine, art, social work, agriculture and many others. Behind all these impulses, however, lies the path of inner schooling, which enables the individual human being to fructify every sphere of life to which he actively applies his energy. This path of inner schooling, which Rudolf Steiner developed out of his own experience, permeates the entire corpus of his life work. Thus each single publication can represent only a small part of a mighty spiritual edifice. During the different phases of his work Rudolf Steiner forged the language and the structures that were appropriate for the substance conveyed.

It is clear, however, that although the language and structures undergo various stages of metamorphosis, the entire work of Rudolf Steiner springs from the source of anthroposophy, from the beginning with his natural-scientific and philosophical writings, throughout all his lecture activity, to the end of his life with the founding of the Anthroposophical Society and the School of Spiritual Science, which continue their active work today throughout the free world.

In this new edition of *Guidance in Esoteric Training* the reader will be able to experience the type of esoteric work which marks the early activity of Rudolf Steiner during the years when his work was contained within the Theosophical Society, although from the beginning as an independent stream. This language with its structures and content may then be compared with excerpts from the lecture of 27 May 1922 which has been included in this edition. Here one finds intensive further illumination on aspects of spiritual training which are present in the early Esoteric School. It is in accordance with Rudolf Steiner's own wish that people who approach his work may do so from as many aspects as possible: 'I try to present spiritual facts again and again from fresh points of view, in spite of my having described them from other points of view in other works. Such accounts are complementary to each other, like photographs of a person or an event taken from various points. In every such description, made from a certain standpoint, there is an opportunity for communicating knowledge which is not attainable from the other points of view.' (Introduction. *The Threshold of the Spiritual World*, Munich, August 1913.)

February 1994

Virginia Sease
Goetheanum
Dornach
Switzerland

Prefatory Note

The contents of this book are selected from the matter of Rudolf Steiner's original Esoteric School. The School remained in existence for ten years from 1904 to 1914, when the outbreak of the First World War prevented its continuance. During that period Rudolf Steiner was still within the Theosophical Society, and he used the words 'theosophy' and 'theosophical', though always (as he tells us in his *Autobiography*) in the direction in which his anthroposophical spiritual science had from the first been pointing. After the lapse of a further ten years, when he went on to found the General Anthroposophical Society and himself became its President, he founded an entirely new worldwide School of Spiritual Science, with a progressive esoteric schooling at its centre and sections relating to the different fields of scientific, artistic and social life. The institution of the Esoteric School in 1904 had been quickly followed by publishing descriptions of the path which pupils should follow, in the book *Theosophy*, in the series of essays *Knowledge of the Higher Worlds: How is it Achieved?* (also entitled *How to Know Higher Worlds*), first published in book form in 1909, and also in *Occult Science: An Outline*, which appeared early in 1910. A description of the basic conditions for inner development, particularly of the 'subsidiary exercises', is also to be found in these books, and after their publication Rudolf Steiner sometimes alluded to such exercises by reference to them. In Chapter V of *Occult Science: An Outline* ('Knowledge of Higher Worlds. Concerning Initiation') he lays down as follows the necessary precondition for *all* the exercises:

> We can however understand from this how necessary it is that man should not demand entry into the spiritual

world until he has learned and understood certain essential truths of that world by the simple exercise of his everyday intelligence, developed in the physical world. If spiritual development follows the right and normal path, then before he aspires to enter the supersensible world the pupil will already have mastered with his ordinary intelligence the whole of the earlier contents of this book.

In 1947, 33 years after the First World War had interrupted the Esoteric School and two years after the end of the Second, Marie Steiner, in response to requests from members of the Anthroposophical Society, set about publishing the most important of the Contents of the Esoteric School. Numerous works on oriental training methods (yoga, etc.) were making their appearance, and it was her object to set against these something from the European discipline of Rudolf Steiner. 'By making available,' she wrote in a letter, 'examples of Rudolf Steiner's careful, personally delivered advice, I wished to ensure that something could come forth from that Rosicrucian stream which is more in tune with the present age than decadent Indian and Tibetan methods.'

Three separate series of selections in English translation, entitled *From the Contents of the Esoteric School*, have previously appeared in 1948, 1949 and 1954. The following includes a revised translation of all that they contain together with some additional material not previously published in English.

Owen Barfield
(revised 1983)

The Task of Spiritual Science

Notes of a lecture given in Berlin in 1903 or 1904

There is a beautiful saying by Hegel: 'The most profound thought is bound up with the historical, external figure of Christ. And the greatness of the Christian religion is that it is there for every stage of development. It is within the grasp of the most naive consciousness and at the same time it is a challenge to the deepest wisdom.'

That the Christian religion is comprehensible to every stage of consciousness is shown by the very history of its development. Properly understood, it must be the task of theosophy, or of spiritual science in general, to show that the Christian religion calls for penetration into the deepest Wisdom teachings. Theosophy is not a religion, but an instrument for understanding the religions. Its relation to the religious documents is rather like the relation of mathematics itself to the writings in which it was originally taught. A man can understand mathematics through his own spiritual faculties and comprehend the laws of space without having to refer to any such early text. But if he has really absorbed the truths of geometry, he will value all the more highly the original texts through which these laws were first presented. So it is with theosophy. Its sources are not in ancient documents, nor do they rest upon tradition; they lie in the reality of the spiritual worlds. It is there that they must be found and grasped by the development of man's own spiritual powers, just as he grasps mathematics by endeavouring to develop the faculties of his intellect. Our intellect, by means of which we are enabled to comprehend the laws of the world of sense, is supported by an organ, the brain. Similarly, in order to grasp the laws of spiritual worlds, we need appropriate organs.

How have our physical organs developed? Because forces from outside have worked upon them: the forces of the sun, the forces of sound. Thus did eyes and ears come into being out of neutral, sluggish organs into which, at first, the sense-world could not penetrate, and which opened only by degrees. If our spiritual organs are worked upon by the right forces, they too will open.

What then are the forces which surge in upon our still inert spiritual organs? During the daytime, the astral body of modern man is assailed by forces that work against his development, and even destroy such organs as he formerly possessed before the dawn of his clear day-consciousness. In earlier times, man received direct astral impressions. The surrounding world spoke to him through pictures, through the form in which the astral world comes to expression. Living, inwardly organic pictures and colours hovered freely in surrounding space as expressions of pleasure and repugnance, sympathy and antipathy. Then these colours wrapped themselves, as it were, round the surface of things, and objects acquired fixed outlines. This was when the physical body of man was steadily gaining in solidity and becoming more highly organized. When his eyes opened fully to the physical light, when the veil of Maya spread itself over the spiritual world, his astral body received impressions of the surrounding world by way of the physical and etheric bodies. The astral body itself transmitted these impressions to the 'I' and from the 'I' they passed into his consciousness. Thus he was personally involved and continuously active. But the forces working upon him were no longer plastic, weaving forces akin to the nature of his own being; they were forces that fed upon him, destroyed him, in order to awaken the 'I'-consciousness. Only in the night, when he sank down into the rhythmic spiritual world homogeneous with him, did he acquire new strength and become able once more to feed forces into his physical and etheric bodies. Out of this conflict of impressions, out of the deadening of the astral organs formerly working unconsciously in man, the life of the individual 'I', the 'I'-consciousness, arose. Out of life — death, out of death — life. The ring of the serpent was complete. And now from the wakened 'I'-consciousness there had to arise forces that would kindle life again in the defunct vestiges of earlier astral organs, shaping and moulding them.

Mankind is moving towards this goal, guided by its Teachers and Leaders, the great Initiates, of whom the serpent is also the symbol. It is an education towards freedom, hence a slow and difficult education. The great Initiates could have made the task easier, for themselves and for man, if they had worked upon his astral body during the night, when it is free, in such a way as to impress the astral organs into it from outside. But such an act would have operated in man's dream-consciousness; it would have trespassed on his sphere of freedom. The highest principle in man, the will, would never have unfolded. Man is led onward stage by stage. There has been an initiation in wisdom, an initiation in feeling, an initiation in will. True Christianity is the summation of all stages of initiation. The initiation of antiquity was the prophetic announcement, the preparation. Slowly and gradually the man of later times emancipated himself from his initiator, his guru. Initiation, to begin with, proceeded in deep trance consciousness, but was equipped to imprint in the physical body a remembrance of what had transpired outside the body. Hence the necessity of releasing the ether body, the bearer of memory, as well as the astral body. Astral body and ether body sank together into the Ocean of Wisdom, into Mahadeva, into the Light of Osiris. This initiation proceeded in deepest secrecy, in absolute seclusion. No breath from the outer world might intrude. The man was as if he had died to outer life, and the tender seeds were nurtured away from the blinding light of day.

Then initiation came forth from the darkness enshrouding the Mysteries into the clearest light of day. In a great and mighty Personality, the Bearer of the highest unifying Principle, of the Word—of Him who is the expression and manifestation of the hidden Father, and who taking on human form became the Son of Man and thereby the Representative of all Mankind, the bond uniting all 'I's—in Christos, the Life-Spirit, the Eternal Unifier, the initiation of mankind as a whole was accomplished as historical fact and at the same time as symbol, on the plane of feeling. So potent was this Event that in every individual who modelled his life on it its power could continue to work—right into the physical, expressing itself even in the appearance of the stigmata and in the most piercing pains. Feelings were shaken to their innermost depths. An intensity of emotion, the like of which has never surged through the world before or since, arose in mighty waves. In the initiation on the Cross of Divine Love, the sacrifice of the 'I' for All had taken place. The blood, the physical expression of the 'I', had flowed in love for mankind, and the effect was such that thousands pressed forward to this initiation, to this Death, letting their blood flow in love and devotion for mankind. That blood untold was poured out in this way has never been sufficiently emphasized; the thought no longer enters the consciousness of people, not even in theosophical circles. Yet the waves of ardour which in this streaming blood flowed down, and then ascended, have fulfilled their task. They have become the wellsprings of powerful impulses. They have made mankind ripe for the initiation of the will.

And this is the legacy of Christ.

I
GENERAL REQUIREMENTS
(SUBSIDIARY EXERCISES)

General Demands which Every Aspirant for Occult Development Must Put to Himself

In what follows, the conditions which must be the basis of any occult development are set forth. Let no one imagine that he can make progress by any measures applied to the outer or the inner life unless he fulfils these conditions. All exercises in meditation, concentration, or exercises of other kinds are valueless, indeed in a certain respect actually harmful, if life is not regulated in accordance with these conditions. No forces can actually be imparted to a human being; all that can be done is to bring to development the forces already within him. They do not develop of their own accord because outer and inner hindrances obstruct them. The outer hindrances are lessened by means of the following rules of life, the inner hindrances by the special instructions concerning meditation, concentration, and the like.

The first condition is the cultivation of absolutely clear thinking. For this purpose a man must rid himself of the will-o'-the-wisps of thought, even if only for a very short time during the day—about five minutes (the longer, the better). He must become the ruler of his world of thought. He is not the ruler if external circumstances, occupation, some tradition or other, social relationships, even membership of a particular race, the daily round of life, certain activities and so forth, determine a thought and how he works it out. Therefore during this brief time, acting entirely out of his own free will, he must empty the soul of the ordinary, everyday courses of thoughts and by his own initiative place one single thought at the centre of his soul. The thought need not be a particularly striking or interesting one. Indeed it will be all the better for what has to be attained in an occult respect if a thoroughly uninteresting and insignificant thought is chosen. Thinking is then impelled to act out of its own energy, the essential thing here, whereas an interesting thought carries the thinking along with it. It is better if this exercise in thought control is undertaken with a pin rather than with Napoleon. The pupil says to himself: Now I start from this thought, and through my own inner initiative I associate with it everything that is pertinent to it. At the end of the period the thought should be just as colourful and living as it was at the beginning. This exercise is repeated day by day for at least a month; a new thought may be taken every day, or the same thought may be adhered to for several days. At the end of the exercise an endeavour is made to become fully conscious of that inner feeling of firmness and security which will soon be noticed by paying subtler attention to one's own soul; the exercise is then brought to a conclusion by focusing the thinking upon the head and the middle of the spine (brain and spinal cord), as if the feeling of security were being poured into this part of the body.

When this exercise has been practised for, say, one month, a second requirement should be added. We try to think of some action that in the ordinary course of life we should certainly not have performed. Then we make it a duty to perform this action every day. It will therefore be good to choose an action that can be performed every day and will occupy as long a period of time as possible. Again it is better to begin with some insignificant action which we have to force ourselves to perform, for example to water at a fixed time every day a flower we have bought. After a certain time a second, similar act should be added to the first, later, a third, and so on ... as many as are compatible with the carrying out of all other duties. This exercise, also, should last for one month. But as far as possible during this second month, too, the first exercise should continue, although it is a less paramount duty than in the first month.

Nevertheless it must not be left unheeded, for otherwise it will quickly be noticed that the fruits of the first month are lost and the slovenliness of uncontrolled thinking begins again. Care must be taken that once these fruits have been won they are never again lost. If, through the second exercise, this initiative of action has been achieved, then, with subtle attentiveness, we become conscious of the feeling of an inner impulse of activity in the soul; we pour this feeling into the body, letting it stream down from the head to a point just above the heart.

In the third month, life should be centred on a new exercise — the development of a certain equanimity towards the fluctuations of joy and sorrow, pleasure and pain; 'heights of jubilation' and 'depths of despair' should quite consciously be replaced by an equable mood. Care is taken that no pleasure shall carry us away, no sorrow plunge us into the depths, no experience lead to immoderate anger or vexation, no expectation give rise to anxiety or fear, no situation disconcert us, and so on. There need be no fear that such an exercise will make life arid and unproductive; far rather will it quickly be noticed that the experiences to which this exercise is applied are replaced by purer qualities of soul. Above all, if subtle attentiveness is maintained, an inner tranquillity in the body will one day become noticeable; as in the two cases above, we pour this feeling into the body, letting it stream from the heart towards the hands, the feet and, finally, the head. This naturally cannot be done after each exercise, for here it is not a matter of one single exercise but of sustained attentiveness to the inner life of the soul. Once every day, at least, this inner tranquillity should be called up before the soul and then the exercise of pouring it out from the heart should proceed. A connection with the exercises of the first and second months is maintained, as in the second month with the exercise of the first month.

In the fourth month, as a new exercise, what is sometimes

called a 'positive attitude' to life should be cultivated. It consists in seeking always for the good, the praiseworthy, the beautiful and the like, in all beings, all experiences, all things. This quality of soul is best characterized by a Persian legend concerning Christ Jesus. One day, as He was walking with His disciples, they saw a dead dog lying by the roadside in a state of advanced decomposition. All the disciples turned away from the disgusting sight; Christ Jesus alone did not move but looked thoughtfully at the corpse and said: 'What beautiful teeth the animal has!' Where the others had seen only the repulsive, the unpleasant, He looked for the beautiful. So must the esoteric pupil strive to seek for the positive in every phenomenon and in every being. He will soon notice that under the veil of something repugnant there is a hidden beauty, that even under the outer guise of a criminal there is a hidden good, that under the mask of a lunatic the divine soul is somehow concealed.

In a certain respect this exercise is connected with what is called 'abstention from criticism'. This is not to be understood in the sense of calling black white and white black. There is, however, a difference between a judgement which, proceeding merely from one's own personality, is coloured with the element of personal sympathy or antipathy, and an attitude which enters lovingly into the alien phenomenon or being, always asking: how has it come to be like this or to act like this? Such an attitude will by its very nature be more set upon helping what is imperfect than upon simply finding fault and criticizing.

The objection that the very circumstances of their lives oblige many people to find fault and condemn is not valid here. For in such cases the circumstances are such that the person in question cannot go through a genuine occult training. There are indeed many circumstances in life that make occult schooling impossible, beyond a certain point. In such a case the person should not impatiently desire, in spite of everything, to make progress that is possible only under some conditions.

He who consciously turns his mind, for one month, to the positive aspect of all his experiences will gradually notice a feeling creeping into him as if his skin were becoming porous on all sides, and as if his soul were opening wide to all kinds of secret and delicate processes in his environment which hitherto entirely escaped his notice. The important point is to combat a very prevalent lack of attentiveness to these subtle things. If it has once been noticed that the feeling described expresses itself in the soul as a kind of bliss, endeavours should be made in thought to guide this feeling to the heart and from there to let it stream into the eyes, and thence out into the space in front of and around oneself. It will be noticed that an intimate relationship to this surrounding space is thereby acquired. A man grows out of and beyond himself, as it were. He learns to regard a part of his environment as something that belongs to him. A great deal of concentration is necessary for this exercise, and, above all, recognition of the fact that all tumultuous feelings, all passions, all over-exuberant emotions have an absolutely destructive effect upon the mood indicated. The exercises of the first months are repeated, as with the earlier months.

In the fifth month, efforts should be made to develop the feeling of confronting every new experience with complete open-mindedness. The esoteric pupil must break entirely with the attitude which, in the face of something just heard or seen, exclaims: 'I never heard that, or I never saw that, before; I don't believe it—it's an illusion.' At every moment he must be ready to encounter and accept absolutely new experiences. What he has hitherto recognized as being in accordance with natural law, or what he has regarded as possible, should present no obstacle to the acceptance of a new truth. Although radically expressed, it is absolutely correct that if anyone were to come to the esoteric pupil and say, 'Since last night the steeple of such and such a church has been tilted right over,' the esotericist should leave a loophole open for the contingency of his becoming convinced that his previous knowledge of natural law could somehow be augmented by such an apparently unprecedented fact.

If he turns his attention, in the fifth month, to developing this attitude of mind, he will notice creeping into his soul a feeling as if something were becoming alive, astir, in the space referred to in connection with the exercise for the fourth month. This feeling is exceedingly delicate and subtle. Efforts must be made to be attentive to his delicate vibration in the environment and to let it stream, as it were, through all the five senses, especially through the eyes, the ears and through the skin, in so far as the latter contains the sense of warmth. At this stage of esoteric development, less attention is paid to the impressions made by these stimuli on the other senses of taste, smell and touch. At this stage it is still not possible to distinguish the numerous bad influences which intermingle with the good influences in this sphere; the pupil therefore leaves this for a later stage.

In the sixth month, endeavours should be made to repeat all the five exercises again, systematically and in regular alternation. In this way a beautiful equilibrium of soul will gradually develop. It will be noticed, especially, that previous dissatisfactions with certain phenomena and beings in the world completely disappear. A mood reconciling all experiences takes possession of the soul, a mood that is by no means one of indifference but, on the contrary, enables one for the first time to work in the world for its genuine progress and improvement. One comes to a tranquil understanding of things that were formerly quite closed to the soul. The very movements and gestures of a person change under the influence of such exercises, and if, one day, he can actually observe that the character of his handwriting has altered, then he may say to himself that he is just about to reach a first rung on the upward path. Once again, two things must be stressed.

First, the six exercises described paralyse the harmful influence other occult exercises can have, so that only what is beneficial remains. Secondly, these exercises alone ensure that efforts in meditation and concentration will have a positive result. The esotericist must not rest content with fulfilling, however conscientiously, the demands of conventional morality, for that kind of morality can be extremely egotistical, if a man says: I will be good in order that I may be thought good. The esotericist does not do what is good because he wants to be thought good, but because little by little he recognizes that the good alone brings evolution forward, and that evil, stupidity and ugliness place hindrances along its path.

Additional Rules in Continuation of the General Requirements

The following rules should provide the esoteric pupil with the means to arrange his life as far as possible in such a way that he can continually watch and govern himself, observing whether he is really allowing himself to be inwardly guided by particular requirements. All esoteric training, particularly when it progresses to higher stages, can lead the pupil only into calamity and confusion if such rules are not observed. But as long as he strives to live in accordance with them he will have no cause to fear embarking on such a training. Neither will he need to lose hope if he should have to say to himself: 'I fulfil this requirement only in a most inadequate way.' It will suffice if he honestly strives, in every area of his life, to remember these rules. Such an honesty must, above all, be an honesty towards oneself. Many deceive themselves in this respect, believing their striving to be a true one. Yet if they would examine themselves more closely they would find a good deal of concealed egoism and refined feelings of self-worth lurking in the background. Such feelings often assume the mask of selfless striving and lead the pupil astray. An earnest inner self-examination cannot be practised often enough, to observe whether one is, after all, harbouring such feelings within one's soul. One can become ever freer of such feelings by energetically following the rules which are presented here. These rules are:

Firstly: *No idea which has not first been examined shall be allowed to enter my consciousness.*

One should occasionally observe how many ideas, feelings and impulses of will live in the soul of a human being, which he adopts as a result of his life-circumstances: his family, profession, nationality, the time in which he lives, etc. There is no need to regard the banishing of such soul-content as a necessary and moral act for every human being. After all, the human being finds certainty and security in life when he is upheld by nationality, time, family, education, etc. If he should thoughtlessly reject such things he would very soon have thrown away all the supports in his life. Particularly for those of a weak disposition it is undesirable to go too far in this direction. Every esoteric pupil should be quite clear that, at the same time as observing this first rule, he also needs to develop an understanding for the deeds, thoughts and feelings of others. By following this rule he should never be led to a lack of restraint or to think that he should break with everything that surrounds him in the form of life-circumstances. On the contrary, the more he examines it, the more he will recognize the legitimacy of what lives in his environment. It is not a question of struggling against and arrogantly rejecting such things, but of becoming inwardly free through a conscientious examination of everything that stands in relationship to one's own soul. The strength of one's own soul will then shed light upon all one's thoughts and conduct; one's consciousness will grow correspondingly broader and one will be able, above all, to form the habit of allowing the spiritual laws which reveal themselves in the soul to express themselves, thus emancipating oneself from a blind obedience to the surrounding world. It could be said, with some apparent justification, that this rule might imply that the pupil must especially scrutinize the occult and esoteric teachings given to him by his esoteric teacher, if he is to examine everything. But one also needs to have a correct understanding of such scrutiny. It is not always possible to investigate something in a direct way; one must find indirect ways of providing oneself with proof. No one today, for example, would be able to establish directly whether Frederick the Great ever lived or not. What can be done, however, is to check whether information about Frederick the Great has reached one through reliable channels. It is the same with all belief based upon the word of an authority. When receiving a communication from someone which one is not in a position to verify directly, one needs to examine the available material to establish whether the person in question is a trustworthy authority, whether the things which he says ring true. This example should demonstrate that scrutiny and proof must start at the right point.

A second rule states: *My soul should be vividly aware of the obligation to increase constantly the sum of my concepts and ideas.*

Nothing is worse for the esoteric pupil than staying fixed with a certain number of concepts and trying to understand everything by means of them. It is infinitely important to be constantly appropriating one new idea after another. If this should not happen, the pupil would be ill-prepared to meet any sense-free perceptions he might develop, and would be overpowered by them either to his disadvantage or at least to his dissatisfaction. To his dissatisfaction, because under such circumstances he could well be having higher experiences already without even noticing it. There are many pupils for whom this is the case, who do not recognize higher experiences because of incorrect expectations due to a paucity of concepts. Many people are not in the least indolent in their outward lives, but are nevertheless quite reluctant to enrich their conceptual life with new ways of understanding.

A third rule is: *I will only gain knowledge about those things to which I am not attached in sympathy or antipathy.*

An old initiate repeatedly drove home this point to his pupils by saying: 'You will only learn something about the soul's immortality when you are as equable about the possibility of its annihilation after death as about the possibility of eternal life. As long as you wish to live eternally you can learn nothing about life after death.' It is the same with all truths. As long as the human being still harbours the slightest wish that things might be one way or another, the pure bright light of truth will not shine for him. Whoever, for example, retains even the most hidden wish that his good qualities might outweigh his bad will not be able to achieve real self-knowledge, for this wish will pull the wool over his inner eyes and deceive him. A fourth rule says: *I am obliged to overcome my reservations towards what seems 'abstract'.*

As long as an esoteric pupil clings on to ideas whose substance is derived from the sense-world, he cannot attain to any truth about higher worlds. He must strive to develop sense-free concepts. This is the hardest rule of all four, particularly in the circumstances of our day and age. Materialistic thinking has to a large extent deprived human beings of the capacity to think in sense-free concepts. One must do one of two things: either strive to think concepts that are never perfectly, but only approximately, present in sensory reality—for example, the concept of a circle. A perfect circle can be nowhere found, but only conceived of; such a conceived circle is the underlying law out of which all circular formations arise. Alternatively, one can think of a high moral ideal; this also cannot be wholly realized by any human being, but it is nevertheless the foundation or law underlying many human deeds. No one can make any progress in their esoteric development if they do not recognize the fundamental importance for life of such so-called abstractions, and enrich their soul with the relevant concepts.

For the Days of the Week

The pupil must pay careful attention to certain activities in the life of soul which in the ordinary way are carried on carelessly and inattentively. There are eight such activities. It is naturally best to undertake *only one exercise* at a time, throughout a week or a fortnight, for example, then the second, and so on, then beginning over again. Meanwhile it is best for the eighth exercise to be carried out every day. True self-knowledge is then gradually achieved and any progress made is perceived. Then later on — beginning with Saturday — one exercise lasting for about five minutes may be added daily so that the relevant exercise will always fall on the same day. Thus: Saturday — Thoughts; Sunday — Resolves; Monday — Talking; Tuesday — Actions; Wednesday — Behaviour, and so on.

SATURDAY

To pay attention to one's *ideas*.

To think only significant thoughts. To learn little by little to separate in one's thoughts the essential from the nonessential, the eternal from the transitory, truth from mere opinion.

In listening to the talk of one's fellow-men, to try and become quite still inwardly, foregoing all assent, and still more all unfavourable judgements (criticism, rejection), even in one's thoughts and feelings.

This may be called

'RIGHT OPINION'

SUNDAY

To determine on even the most insignificant matter only after fully reasoned *deliberation*. All unthinking behaviour, all meaningless actions, should be kept far away from the soul. One should always have well-weighed reasons for everything. And one should definitely abstain from doing anything for which there is no significant reason.

Once one is convinced of the rightness of a decision, one must hold fast to it, with inner steadfastness.

This may be called

'RIGHT JUDGEMENT'

having been formed independently of sympathies and antipathies.

MONDAY

Talking. Only what has sense and meaning should come from the lips of one striving for higher development. All talking for the sake of talking — to kill time — is in this sense harmful.

The usual kind of conversation, a disjointed medley of remarks, should be avoided. This does not mean shutting oneself off from intercourse with one's fellows; it is precisely then that talk should gradually be led to significance. One adopts a thoughtful attitude to every speech and answer, taking all aspects into account. Never talk without cause — be gladly silent. One tries not to talk too much or too little. First listen quietly; then reflect on what has been said.

This exercise may be called

'RIGHT WORD'

TUESDAY

External actions. These should not be disturbing for our fellow men. Where an occasion calls for action out of one's inner being, deliberate carefully how one can best meet the occasion—for the good of the whole, the lasting happiness of man, the eternal.

Where one does things of one's own accord, out of one's own initiative, consider most thoroughly beforehand the effect of one's actions.

This is called

'RIGHT DEED'

WEDNESDAY

The ordering of life. To live in accordance with nature and spirit. Not to be swamped by the external trivialities of life. To avoid all that brings unrest and haste into life. To hurry over nothing, but also not to be indolent. To look on life as a means for working towards higher development and to behave accordingly.

One speaks in this connection of

'RIGHT STANDPOINT'

THURSDAY

Human endeavour. One should take care to do nothing that lies beyond one's powers—but also to leave nothing undone that lies within them.

To look beyond the everyday, the momentary, and to set oneself aims and ideals connected with the highest duties of a human being. For instance, in the sense of the prescribed exercises, to try to develop oneself so that afterwards one may be able all the more to help and advise one's fellow men—though perhaps not in the immediate future.

This can be summed up as

*'TO LET ALL THE FOREGOING EXERCISES
BECOME A HABIT'*

FRIDAY

The endeavour to *learn as much as possible from life*. Nothing goes by us without giving us a chance to gain experiences that are useful for life. If one has done something wrongly or imperfectly, that becomes a motive for doing it rightly or more perfectly, later on. If one sees others doing something, one observes them with the like end in view (yet not coldly or heartlessly). And one does nothing without looking back to past experience which can be of assistance in one's decisions and achievements. One can learn from everyone—even from children if one is attentive.
This exercise is called

'RIGHT MEMORY'
(Remembering what has been learnt from experiences.)

SUMMARY

To turn one's gaze inwards from time to time, even if only for five minutes daily at the same time. In so doing one should sink down into oneself, carefully take counsel with oneself, test and form one's principles of life, run through in thought one's knowledge—or lack of it—weigh up one's duties, think over the contents and true purpose of life, feel genuinely pained by one's own errors and imperfections. In a word: labour to discover the essential, the enduring, and earnestly aim at goals in accord with it—for instance, virtues to be acquired. (Not to fall into the mistake of thinking that one has done something well, but to strive ever further towards the highest standards.)
This exercise is called

'RIGHT EXAMINATION'

For the Months of the Year

The Twelve Virtues. Monthly virtues to be meditated upon and observed in one's life.

April	Devotion	becomes the power of sacrifice
May	Equilibrium	becomes progress
June	Perseverance	becomes faithfulness
July	Unselfishness	becomes catharsis
August	Compassion	becomes freedom
September	Courtesy	becomes steadiness of feeling
October	Contentment	becomes self-composure
November	Patience	becomes understanding
December	Control of speech and thinking (minding one's tongue)	becomes a feeling for the truth
January	Courage	becomes the power of redemption
February	Discretion	becomes the power of meditation
March	Magnanimity	becomes love

These exercises should always be begun on the 21st of the preceding month, e.g. April: from 21 March to 21 April.

II
MAIN EXERCISE

Main Exercise

(*October 1906*)

First thing in the morning, immediately after waking, before any other impressions have passed through the soul, the pupil gives himself up to his meditation. He strives for complete inner stillness, which means that all attention is withdrawn from impressions coming from outside and from all memories of everyday life. He also endeavours to free the soul from all cares and anxieties, which are apt to oppress it particularly at this time. Then the meditation begins. In order to facilitate this inner stillness, the consciousness is first of all directed to a single idea, perhaps that of 'Rest', and then this idea is allowed to disappear from consciousness so that no image whatsoever remains in the soul; the content of the following seven lines is then allowed to live in the soul, to the exclusion of everything else. These seven lines must be held in the consciousness for five minutes. If other images intrude, the pupil keeps returning again to these seven lines, in profound contemplation:

> In purest outpoured Light
> Shimmers the Godhead of the World.
> In purest Love towards all that is
> Outpours the godhood of my soul.
> I rest within the Godhead of the world;
> There shall I find myself,
> Within the Godhead of the world.

> *In den reinen Strahlen des Lichtes*
> *Erglänzt die Gottheit der Welt.*
> *In der reinen Liebe zu allen Wesen*
> *Erstrahlt die Göttlichkeit meiner Seele.*

Ich ruhe in der Gottheit der Welt;
Ich werde mich selbst finden
In der Gottheit der Welt.

After this has been practised for five minutes, the pupil goes on to the following.

He takes a calm, strong breath; after the in-breathing he breathes out, just as calmly and strongly, so that there is no pause between the in-breathing and the out-breathing. Then he abstains from breathing for a brief period, endeavouring however to let the breath remain wholly outside the body. The following are the approximate periods to be observed. The time taken by the in-breathing is optional, to be adjusted in accordance with one's capacities. The out-breathing should take twice as long as the in-breathing, and the abstention from breathing three times as long as the in-breathing. If, for example, two seconds are needed for in-breathing, then four seconds are taken for the out-breathing, and six seconds for the abstention from breathing. This in-breathing, out-breathing, abstention from breathing is repeated *four times*. During the in-breathing and the out-breathing the mind is emptied of thought and the whole consciousness directed to the breathing. But during the first abstention from breathing the pupil concentrates on the point lying between and a little behind the eyebrows, at the root of the nose, inside the forepart of the brain, while he fills his consciousness exclusively with the words:

I am.

During the second abstention from breathing he concentrates on a point inside the larynx, while he fills his consciousness exclusively with the image:

It thinks.

During the third abstention from breathing he concentrates on the two arms and hands. The hands are either held folded, or the right is laid over the left. At the same time he fills his consciousness exclusively with the image:

She feels.

During the fourth abstention from breathing he concentrates on the whole surface of the body; that is, he pictures his bodily self with the utmost possible clarity and fills his consciousness with the image:

He wills.

If these exercises in concentration are continued strenuously for several weeks, something will be felt at those points upon which the consciousness has been focused: at the root of the nose, in the larynx, a stream in the hands and arms and on the whole outer surface of the body.

During concentration upon the arms and hands the pupil will feel as if a force were driving the hands apart; he lets them go apart, following the line of the force, but he does not suggest this to himself. The feeling must come quite of itself.

In 'It thinks', the 'It' signifies the universal Cosmic Thinking which should live as impersonal power in our words. In 'She feels', the 'She' signifies the Cosmic Soul—it means that we should feel, not personally but impersonally, in the sense that the Cosmic Soul is impersonal. In 'He wills', the 'He' signfies God, within whose will we instate our whole being.

When the pupil has carried through these four breathing exercises, he fills his consciousness for a while with one *single* image in which he is entirely absorbed, so that during this time nothing else whatever is present in the soul.

This image is given by Rudolf Steiner differently to individual pupils depending on their personality. For example:

'My Power'
or 'I in me'
or 'I will'
or 'I am steadfast'
or 'Quietness in the strength
Strength in the quietness'
or 'Warmth of soul entirely fills me'.

Then we pass on to complete absorption, for five minutes, in our own divine ideal. This exercise must be enacted with the utmost devotion and reverence.

The whole meditation need not last longer than 15 minutes. In all the periods specified above, we do not go by the clock but by our feeling. Care is taken to adopt such a position of the body that the body itself cannot (because of fatigue, for instance) be a cause of distraction.

The previous mantra in a rather more individualized form:

In purest outpoured Light
Shimmers the Godhead of the world.
In purest ether fire
Outpours the lofty Power that is 'I'.
I rest within the Spirit of the World,
There shall I find myself for ever,
In the Eternal Spirit of the world.

In den reinen Strahlen des Lichtes
Erglänzt die Gottheit der Welt.
In dem reinen Feuer des Äthers
Erstrahlt der Ichheit hohe Kraft.
Ich ruhe im Geiste der Welt,
Ich werde mich immer finden
Im ewigen Geiste der Welt.

1. Here is a morning meditation which is to be carried out as follows.

First thing in the morning before embarking on any kind of everyday activity and before taking any food the pupil should establish a state of complete quietness of soul.

Attention is withdrawn from any external sense impressions and from all habitual ideas of the intellect. All memories of ordinary experiences must also be completely still. Above all, any anxieties and cares relating to one's life must be silenced entirely.

Out of the entirely quietened soul the single idea must then arise:

Above, all as below
Below, all as above

For ten minutes (not by the clock but according to one's feeling) the pupil must now live strictly in images that can be won from this idea by applying it to the manifestations of the world. These images need not necessarily all be entirely correct; the important thing is to develop the images in this general direction. However, every effort should be made to ensure that solely correct images are thought.

When this has been completed the pupil then moves on to the following: seven breaths are taken, the length of the inhalation being such that the rest of the exercise can be accomplished without causing any harm.

Take a breath; when you have finished inhaling breathe out again immediately and then let the air remain outside, so that for a period inhalation is suppressed.

Keep to the following timing.

Inhalation: to be judged as indicated above.

Exhalation: twice as long as the inhalation.

Abstention from breathing in again: four times as long as the inhalation. (This applies to the beginning; gradually this is increased to ten times as long as the inhalation.)

During the first and second abstention from breathing the pupil immerses himself entirely in the image:

I am

and concentrates on the point at the root of the nose. (This point is arrived at by taking the point between the eyebrows and drawing a horizontal line backwards from there; it is about one centimetre back.)

During the third and fourth abstention from breathing the pupil must immerse himself in the image:

It thinks

while concentrating on the larynx.

During the fifth and sixth abstention from breathing the pupil must immerse himself in the image:

She feels

while concentrating on the heart.

During the seventh abstention from breathing you immerse yourself in:

He wills

while concentrating on the navel by thinking of rays radiating out from it through the whole of the abdomen.

There is no thinking while inhaling and exhaling. ('*It*' signifies the universal Cosmic Thinking. '*She*' signifies the Cosmic Soul. '*He*' signifies the Cosmic Spirit. However, these images are only for orientation; they should not be present in one's consciousness during the meditation. They would only distract from the mantric character of the above formulation.)

To conclude this exercise, the pupil, in a mood of devotion, immerses himself in his own divine ideal for five minutes.

2. During the course of the day the subsidiary exercises described separately are carried out.
3. In the evening the events of the day are reviewed backwards.

Alcohol must be strictly avoided. A vegetarian diet is helpful but not essential.

Explanation of the Foregoing Main Exercise

Whoever strives for esoteric development must above all be clear that certain extremely simple formulae conceal a force that takes effect if these formulae or sentences are made alive in the soul. He does not rightly grasp what this implies if he tries to understand such sentences merely with the intellect. That way they say very little to him, to begin with. He must for a certain time fill his whole inner being with such a sentence, pouring himself into it with all the powers of his soul. Such a sentence is: *I am*.

The whole secret of present-day human existence really lies in this sentence. Only a being possessed of an external form similar to that of earthly man today is able to think, feel and imbue these words with will. The form of such a being must have developed in such a way that the goal of all the forces working in the body was the frontward shape of the vaulted brow. This vaulted brow and the 'I am' belong together. Earlier in the evolution of the human form there was a stage when it had not yet pressed forward into such a brow. At that time the 'I am' could be neither inwardly thought, nor willed, nor felt. Now it would be quite wrong to believe that the form of the body, as described above, could itself bring forth the 'I am'. This 'I am' was already in existence, only it could not yet express itself in an appropriate form. Just as it now expresses itself in the bodily form of man, so, in an earlier time, it expressed itself in a world of soul. And it is this very power of the 'I am' which, having united in the far distant past with a human body lacking the present brow-formation, impelled the forehead to assume its present shape. Hence it is that a man, by sinking deeply into the 'I am', can feel within himself the force which has moulded him in his present form. And this force is higher than the forces which, in his ordinary life, are active within him today. For it is the creative force of soul which forms the bodily nature out of the soul.

Anyone, therefore, who is aiming at esotericism must, for a short period, live entirely in the 'I am'. He must think this 'I am', while at the same time he experiences within himself something like: 'I rejoice that I, as an independent being, can participate in the work of shaping the world.' And he must also experience something like: 'I will my own existence; I resolve to place myself in the whole context of the world.' If a man concentrates all this into a single, inner act of consciousness, and at the same time shifts the whole force of his consciousness upwards into the region of the brow and the inner members of the brain beneath it, then he actually transfers himself into a higher world out of which his brow formation has been brought into being.

Let him not think, however, that he can attain these higher worlds tomorrow morning. He must have a patience to undertake this meditation day by day, over and over again, for a long time. If he has this patience, then, after some time, he will notice a thought arising within him — no longer a mere concept but a thought teeming with life and force. He will be able to say to himself: 'The force contained in the seed of a plant, impelling it to form the organs of the plant, must be inwardly alive, just like this thought of mine.' And soon this thought will reveal itself to him as if it were radiating light. In this inner radiation of light he feels happy, full of the joy of existence. A feeling permeates him which can only be described as 'joyful love in creative existence'. And a force imparts itself to the will as if the thought were radiating warmth through the will, energizing the will. All this can be drawn from sinking himself in the right way into the 'I am'. He will gradually realize that the highest intellectual, psychical and moral power comes to birth in him in this way, and that he thereby brings himself into a more and more conscious relationship to a higher world.

A second such sentence is: '*It thinks*'. This 'It thinks' represents — in a way that corresponds to the account given of the 'I am' — the force through which the form of the human speech-organs has been developed from the higher worlds. When thinking was still functioning in a higher world of soul, and not yet within a human body, it worked from that higher world in such a way that organs of speech not yet existing in the human form were incorporated into it. If, therefore, the esoteric pupil sends his thinking, feeling and willing into the depths of the 'It thinks', at the same time concentrating his consciousness on the region of the larynx, there will arise in him an experience of the creative force of soul which, from the higher worlds, manifested in the creation of the organs of speech. If again he has the patience described above, he will experience how from the 'It thinks' rays go forth which are like the opening harmonies of spiritual music; they fill him with a feeling of reverent devotion, and at the same time with a force which tells him: 'What I *will*, as man, will gradually increase in wisdom.' An inkling will come to him of that force which as divine-spiritual force pours itself through the cosmos, ordering all things according to measure, number and weight.

A third sentence is '*She feels*'. In still earlier times, the force of this sentence, too, was not yet present within man but dwelt in a higher world of soul. Working down from that higher world, it re-cast the form of the human body. Until then there had been no difference between hands and feet; they were identically shaped organs of movement. Hence man had not yet attained his upright posture. It was a great step forward in human evolution when his anterior organs of movement were transformed into organs for manual work. He was then able to assume his upright posture and so to overcome his lower nature, inasmuch as his gaze was now directed out and upwards towards the heavenly worlds of spirit. Thereby, too, he first became capable of fashioning karma. For it is only when a being possesses this particular form that his deeds come within his own, individual responsibility.

Thus it was that spiritual Beings transformed man, as the force of the 'She feels', which had previously reposed in them alone, streamed into the human body. If therefore the esoteric pupil sinks himself into the 'She feels', again in the way described above, he raises himself to the corresponding Creative Powers of the higher worlds. But together with the 'She feels' he must concentrate the whole of his consciousness on his arms and hands. Out of the thought 'She feels' an experience of indescribably blissful life will then stream to him. This feeling can be described as that of 'love in active existence'. Thereby he attains consciousness of how the Creative Love flows through cosmic space, and by its deed pours into all things the breath of life.

A fourth sentence is *'He wills'*. It was by the force of this sentence that in a primeval past the human body, as a whole, was for the first time separated out as an independent being from its environment.

Before this force worked upon it from higher worlds, the human body was not shut off on all sides by an outer skin. Streams of substance flowed into the body from all sides and out of it again. It had no independent life but was entirely immersed in the life of its environment. In that epoch, of course, the environment was quite different from that of our own time. If the esoteric pupil now again sinks all his thinking, feeling and willing into the 'He wills', concentrating his consciousness on the whole surface of the outer skin, he transfers himself gradually into the sublime creative forces of the 'He wills'. These are the forces of the supersensible world whereby the things of the world of sense are given their form and shape. If he has sufficient endurance, the human being will feel, in the deeply inward experience of this thought, as if he were raised above all sensible-corporeal existence and were looking down upon the field of sense-creation in order to work upon it in conformity with the Divine Thoughts attained in the spiritual world. The force proceeding from this thought is that of being joyously transported into pure spirituality, and the attainment of a consciousness that out of higher regions one can bring to the world of sense that of which it stands in need.

As he engrosses himself deeply in these thoughts that are forces, the esotericist will simultaneously have to focus attention on his breathing-process and, for a short time, transform it from an unconscious process into a consciously regulated act. For while the forces working from higher worlds upon the human form were achieving the transformation indicated, these same forces produced, within this form, the present breathing-system—the system necessary for a being whose body has an independent existence, the work of whose hands is his own responsibility, whose organs of speech can translate experiences in the life of soul into externally audible sounds. The ascent into the higher regions of world-creation is furthered by directing the attention in this way to the breathing process.

If the esoteric pupil learns by degrees thus to experience consciously the higher cosmic forces, which indeed are always slumbering within him but of which he has hitherto been unaware, then what he should already have assimilated through study becomes alive in him, begins to glimmer into perceptible reality. He should already have acquired the knowledge that man, together with the evolution of the earth as a whole, passed through different stages of transformation before the present earth came into being. These stages of transformation are called: the Saturn condition, the Sun condition, the Moon condition. The esotericist has also to acquire the knowledge that in later epochs there is a certain recapitulation of earlier conditions.

Thus the Saturn, Sun and Moon conditions were recapitulated during the Earth-evolution, and in such a way that the Saturn repetition corresponds to the creative work of the 'He wills' on the outer sheath of the human being. The Sun recapitulation corresponds to the creative work of the 'She feels' on the arms and hands, and the Moon recapitulation to the creative work of the 'It thinks' on the organs of speech. The idea of the human body as a mere product of the sense-world is abandoned, and the esotericist finds his way to vision of those higher worlds whence come the forces that work creatively upon man. So, too, the bare concepts which have been acquired of such matters as Saturn, Sun and Moon become actual perceptions and experiences. And so indeed it must be if the way is to be found more and more from the exoteric to the esoteric.

The exercises given here must of course be regarded only as a beginning. The pupil must, however, work strenuously through them, and then he will reach the point where he can receive the further exercises through which still higher forces that slumber within him are awakened. The aim is to gain an inkling of the spiritual facts that underline the words 'I am', 'It thinks', 'She feels', 'He wills', and to feel their connection with the members of the human body, whose form has arisen from out of the spiritual world.

It should be added, for information, that in the above Words of Power, the three forms

IT — SHE — HE

are well founded in the nature of the higher worlds.

'It' is the Word of Power for the Cosmic Thinking, that is, for those Beings in the higher world to whom creative thinking belongs in just the same measure as sense-perception belongs to the human beings below them.

'She' is the Word of Power for the Cosmic Soul which originates the Feeling that streams out from it, whereas human feeling streams in, being stimulated from outside.

This Feeling of the World Soul is the Creative Cosmic Love, which brings all things into existence.

'He' is the Word of Power for the Cosmic Will, the Cosmic Spirit whose will acts from out of Himself, whereas the human will is brought into action through the outer world. This 'He' is the creative, archetypal Power of the World.

Main Exercises Given Individually to Various Pupils

I

Main Exercise for morning and evening.

Morning, as soon as possible after waking:

Withdrawal of attention from all external sense impressions, also from all memories of everyday life. The soul is then filled with the image *Rest.* It should be as if this feeling of Rest were pervading the whole body. This can occupy a very brief time with the following seven lines:

Light-streaming Archetypes	*Lichterstrahlende Gebilde*
Flashing and quivering	*Glänzendes Wogenmeer*
Ocean-floor of Spirit,	* des Geistes,*
My soul deserted you.	*Euch verliess die Seele.*
In the Divine	*In dem Göttlichen*
she stayed awhile,	* weilte sie,*
And therein had her rest.	*In ihm ruhte ihr Wesen.*
Into the zone that wraps	*In das Reich der*
existence round	* Daseinshüllen*
Enters my conscious 'I'.	*Tritt bewusst mein 'Ich'.*

The effort is made to envisage these lines as pictorially as possible. With the first two lines, the image is of an Ocean of Light in which forms are taking shape. With the third, fourth and fifth lines, the image is of how the soul, on waking, emerges from this Ocean of Light. With the sixth and seventh lines, the image is of how man, when he wakes, passes into the sheaths of the body.

The subsidiary exercises are to be carried out during the course of the day. For these exercises it is less essential to adhere to a specific time.

Evening:

'Throughout the day I have received impressions of the outer physical world of sense and have formed ideas about them. During the night I shall have no such impressions. I shall be within the spiritual world. In sense-images I will now picture to myself the supersensible world, so that these sense-images may gradually lead me into this supersensible world. I will see with my mind's eye the space around me and within me filled with supersensible light, as if an ocean of light were pervaded by streaming currents of warmth; one of the streams of warmth enters my heart.' (Light— symbol of Divine Wisdom; warmth—symbol of Divine Love.)

Hold this picture meditatively in complete restfulness of soul, for three to four minutes, and then hold firmly in the soul the lines, but now with the images in reverse sequence:

My conscious 'I' departs	*Es tritt bewusst mein Ich*
Leaving the wrappings	*Aus dem Reich*
of existence	*der Daseinshüllen.*
To rest in wider Being	*Zu ruhen in*
of the Worlds.	*der Welten Wesen.*
Into Divinity it strains.	*Ins Göttliche strebet es.*
Gain, O my soul this Bourne;	*Gewinne Seele dieses Reich;*
The flashing, quivering	*Des Geistes glänzend*
Ocean of the Spirit,	*Wogenmeer*
The shining Archetypes	*Des Lichts erstrahlende*
of Light.	*Gebilde.*

Then a view of the life of the day, in pictures, and in backward order.

II

Evening:

Experience in symbols of the content of light, warmth; then:

Within the Godhead of the World,
There shall I find myself
Wherein I rest.
The godhood of my soul outpours
In purest love towards all that is,
Shimmers the Godhead of the World
In purest light outpoured.

In der Gottheit der Welt
Werde ich mich selber finden,
In IHR ruhe ich.
Es erstrahlt die Göttlichkeit meiner Seele
In der reinen Liebe zu allen Wesen,
Es erglänzt die Gottheit der Welt
In den reinen Strahlen des Lichts.

(Five minutes given to this exercise, then a review backwards over the events of the day—seven to eight minutes.)

Picturing the Rose Cross   *Vorstellung des Rosenkreuzes*

Within my heart let dwell   *In meinem Herzen*
   the Light of Worlds.   *wohne Weltenlicht.*

Morning:

Reawakening of the pictures.

In purest outpoured light
Shimmers the Godhead of the World.
In purest love towards all that is
Outpours the godhood of my soul.
I rest within the Godhead of the World;
There shall I find myself
Within the Godhead of the World.

In den reinen Strahlen des Lichts
Erglänzt die Gottheit der Welt.
In der reinen Liebe zu allen Wesen
Erstrahlt die Göttlichkeit meiner Seele.
Ich ruhe in der Gottheit der Welt;
Ich werde mich selbst finden
In der Gottheit der Welt.

(Five minutes given to this exercise. Then: restfulness of soul.)

Picturing a growing plant, letting it grow slowly before one in thought: leaf by leaf, blossom, fruit. One is to imagine the force whereby the growth is brought about; then to think this force into one's own heart.

(Concentration on this for two to three minutes.)

Within my heart let dwell the Cosmic Word.

In meinem Herzen wohne Weltenwort.

During the day: subsidiary exercises.

III

Evening:

Meditation on the Rose Cross

This symbol shows me
Life's triumph over powerful death.
I will feel in myself
The meaning of this symbol.
It will raise me upright
And upright bear me on
In all the spheres of life.

Es weiset diese Zeichen mir
Lebenssieg über Todesmacht
In mir fühlen will ich
Dieses Zeichens Sinn.
Es wird mich aufrichten
Und aufgerichtet tragen
In allen Lebenssphären.

Morning:

In the Beginning was the Word
And may the Word be in me;
And the Word was Divine.
And with Divine Power
May the Word pervade me.
And a God was the Word
And may the Power of God impart the Word to my will.

Im Urbeginne war das Wort
Und das Wort sei in mir;
Und das Wort war göttlich.
Und mit göttlicher Kraft
Durchdringe mich das Wort.
Und ein Gott war das Wort
Und Gotteskraft gebe das Wort meinem Willen.

By day, the subsidiary exercises.

IV

Evening:

The mind pictures the Rose Cross.

Thou my soul,	*Du meine Seele,*
Look up to this symbol:	*Blicke hin auf dieses Zeichen:*
May it be to thee the sign	*Ausdruck sei es dir*
Of the World Spirit	*Des Weltengeistes,*
Who fills the cosmic spaces,	*Der erfüllet Weltenweiten,*
Who works through	*Der da wirkt durch*
the cycles of time	*Zeitenfolgen*
And works eternally in thee.	*Und ewig wirkt in dir.*
(Restfulness of soul)	*(Seelenruhe)*

Morning:

The mind pictures the Rose Cross.

Let my thinking,	*In diesem Zeichen*
Let my willing,	*Stehe mein Denken,*
Let my feeling,	*Stehe mein Wollen,*
Stand in this sign.	*Stehe mein Fühlen.*
May its meaning	*Was es deutet*
Live in my heart's depths,	*Lebe in meines Herzens Tiefen,*
Live in me as light.	*Lebe als Licht in mir.*
(Restfulness of soul)	*(Seelenruhe)*

V

Evening:

1. Look back on the events of the day, as indicated in the book *Knowledge of the Higher Worlds*. About five minutes.

2. The Rose Cross meditation—about five minutes, and then these lines, again about five minutes:

In the clear rays of the Light	*In des Lichtes reinen Strahlen*
I see in purity	*Kann ich schauen*
The fountain of all wisdom.	*Aller Weisheit reine Kraft.*
In the wave-beat of the heart	*In des Herzens Wellenschlag*
I feel in strength	*Kann ich fühlen*
The token of all Being.	*Alles Daseins Starkes Sinnbild.*
Both of these will I feel.	*Beides will ich fühlen.*
(Restfulness of soul)	*(Seelenruhe)*

Morning:

First, the Rose Cross meditation. Then dwell upon this thought:

Wisdom in the spirit,	*Weisheit im Geiste,*
Love in the soul,	*Liebe in der Seele,*
Strength in the will:	*Kraft im Willen:*
These shall guide me,	*Sie geleiten mich*
These shall hold me.	*Und halten mich.*
In them I trust.	*Ich vertraue ihnen,*
To them I give my life.	*Ich opfre ihnen.*
(Restfulness of soul)	*(Seelenruhe)*

Supplementary exercises as given in *Occult Science: An Outline.*

VI

Evening:

Clear rays of light—	*Des Lichtes reine Strahlen*
Spirit of the World,	*Zeiget mir*
reveal to me!	*der Welten Geist;*
Pure warmth of love—	*Der Liebe reine Wärme*
Soul of the World,	*Zeige mir*
impart to me!	*der Welten Seele.*
Nearness to God	*Gottinnigkeit*
Be in my heart,	*In meinem Herzen*
Be in my spirit.	*In meinem Geist.*
(Restfulness of soul)	*(Seelenruhe)*

Morning:

The mind pictures the Rose Cross.

Be in my spirit,	*In meinem Geist*
Be in my heart,	*In meinem Herzen*
Nearness to God.	*Gottinnigkeit.*
Soul of the World,	*Zeige mir*
impart to me	*der Welten Seele*
Pure warmth of love!	*Der Liebe reine Wärme;*
Spirit of the World,	*Zeiget mir*
reveal to me	*der Welten Geist*
Clear rays of light!	*Des Lichtes reine Strahlen.*
(Restfulness of soul)	*(Seelenruhe)*

VII

Evening:

Look back on the events of the day from evening till morning. Picture the blue orb of heaven, with the great multitude of stars:

With silent reverence	*Fromm und ehrfürchtig*
Into the depths	*Sende ahnend*
of space	*in Raumesweiten*
Go forth the vision	*Meine Seele*
of my soul,	*den fühlenden Blick.*
Thence to receive	*Aufnehme dieser Blick*
And pour into my heart	*Und sende in*
Light and love and life	*meines Herzens Tiefen*
From spiritual worlds.	*Licht, Liebe, Leben,*
(Restfulness of soul)	*Aus Geisteswelten.*
	(Seelenruhe)

Morning:

The mind pictures the Rose Cross.

What through this emblem	*Was in diesem Sinnbild*
The Spirit of the World	*Zu mir spricht*
Is speaking to my heart—	*Der Welten hoher Geist,*
May it imbue my soul	*Erfülle meine Seele*
At all times,	*Zu aller Zeit*
In all contingencies,	*In allen Lebenslagen*
With light and love and life.	*Mit Licht, Liebe, Leben.*
(Restfulness of soul)	*(Seelenruhe)*

VIII

Morning:

The sun is dawning,
The stars disappear.
The soul is dawning,
The dreams disappear,
    Day receive me,
    Day protect me,
    In wayward earthly life.

Es dämmert die Sonne,
Es schwinden die Sterne.
Es dämmert die Seele,
Es schwinden die Träume,
    Tag nimm mich auf.
    Tag beschütze mich
    In wandelndem Erdenleben.

Evening:

When starry Cosmic Being
Withdraws my 'I' in sleep
Into the world of spirit:
    I bring back strength of soul
    From active Cosmic Power,
    To strive towards the Spirit

Wenn Sternenweltensein
Mein Ich ins Geistgebiet
Schlafend entrückt:
    Hole ich mir Seelenkraft
    Aus wirkender Weltenmacht
    Zu streben geisteswärts.

IX

Words of meditation for those already more advanced, laying hold of the feeling:

Evening:

1. Backward review
2. Imagining oneself in the space illuminated by the moon at night; therein one experiences with *feeling*:

In the Beginning was Yahveh	*Im Urbeginn war Jahve*
And Yahveh was with	*Und Jahve war bei*
the Elohim	*den Elohim*
And Yahveh was one of	*Und Jahve war einer*
the Elohim	*der Elohim*
And Yahveh lives in me.	*Und Jahve lebt in mir.*

Then in imagination one lets the moon-illumined space change into the space lit up by the sun by day; therein one experiences with *feeling*:

And Christ lives in me	*Und Christus lebt in mir*
And Christ is one of	*Und Christus ist einer*
the Elohim	*der Elohim*
And Christ is with the Elohim	*Und Christus ist bei den Elohim*
At the end, Christ will be.	*Am Ende wird sein Christus.*

Morning:

First, the sunlit space of day—experience in feeling, in the mood of evening twilight:

At the end will be Christ.

Then imagine the sun overhead:

And Christ is in me.

Then imagine the space of day—experience in feeling, in the mood of morning:

And I am in a 'Christ-ened' world.

In addition: six subsidiary exercises.

X

Evening:

It soars aloft
From cosmic depths,
The Sun of Christ.
Its Light is Spirit.
It shines in the All
It is Spirit in me,
It lives within my 'I'.

Es schwebet empor
Aus den Weltentiefen
Die Christussonne
Ihr Licht wird Geist –
Es leuchtet im All
Es geistet in mir
Es lebet in meinem Ich.

Morning:

It lives within my 'I',
It is Spirit in me,
It shines in the All.
It is the Spirit-Light,
It is the Christ
   Sun's Light
Out of the cosmic depths
Whence, soaring,
   it comes.

Es lebet in meinem Ich
Es geistet in mir
Es leuchtet im All
Es ist das Geisteslicht –
Es ist Licht
   der Christussonne
Aus den Weltentiefen,
Aus denen
   es schwebend kommt.

XI

Evening:

In the Beginning was	*Im Urbeginne war*
the Word	*das Wort*
And the Word was with God	*Und das Wort war bei Gott*
And a God was the Word.	*Und ein Gott war das Wort.*
And the Word,	*Und das Wort,*
May it dwell in thy heart	*Es lebe im Herzen,*
In the heart of thy being—	*Im Herzen deines Wesens,*
In thine 'I'.	*In deinem Ich.*

Morning:

In thine 'I',	*In deinem Ich,*
In the heart of thy being	*Im Herzen deines Wesens*
There lives the Word,	*Da lebe das Wort,*
The Spirit-Word	*Das Geisteswort.*
And the Word was with God	*Und das Wort war bei Gott*
And a God was the Word.	*Und ein Gott was das Wort.*
In the Beginning	*Im Urbeginne*
was the Word.	*war das Wort.*

XII

In the mornings:

Steadfastness	left leg
Certainty	right leg
Love	left hand
Hope	right hand
Trust	head

Steadfastly to take my place on earth	concentrate on left leg
Certain as I walk through life	concentrate on right leg
Love in the core of my being	concentrate on left arm
Hope in all I do	concentrate on right arm
Trust in all my thinking	concentrate on head

These *five* take me to my goal
These *five* give me life on earth.

In the evenings:

Look back on the day's events.
Starting from the end of the day,
as fluid and mobile as possible.

XIII

Another version of the previous exercise:

In the mornings:

Steadfastness	left leg
Certainty	right leg
Strength	heart
Love	left hand
Hope	right hand
Trust	head

Steadfastly I take my place on earth	concentrate on left leg
Certain as I walk through life	concentrate on right leg
Strength pours into my heart	concentrate on the heart
Love in the core of my being	concentrate on left arm
Hope in all I do	concentrate on right arm
Trust in all my thinking	concentrate on head

These *six* go with me through life.

In the evenings:

Look back on the day's events.
Fluid and mobile.
Start from the end of the day.

III
MANTRAS

Meditations which Express the Time Substance of the Hierarchies

Daily Verses

On Friday practise the verse for Saturday, and so on. You can do it several times during the day, and try to spend 20–30 minutes in the depth of such a verse. You will gain very much through this for the achievement of a relationship with the mystery of the all-permeating sevenfoldness.

The day begins in the occult sense at 6 p.m.

FRIDAY FOR SATURDAY

Great all-encompassing Spirit,
    Thou whose existence filled infinite space,
    when of my bodily members
    naught was present as yet.
Thou wert.
    I lift up my soul into Thee.
I was in Thee.
    I was a part of Thy power.
Thou didst send out Thy forces,
    and in the first beginnings of the Earth
    was mirrored my body's original form.
Within Thine out-sent forces
    was I myself.
Thou wert.
On Thee did my archetype gaze,
It gazed on me myself,
    I who was a part of Thee.
Thou wert.

FREITAG FÜR SAMSTAG

Grosser umfassender Geist,
    der Du den endlosen Raum erfülltest,
    als von meinen Leibesgliedern
    Keines noch vorhanden war.
Du warst.
    Ich erhebe meine Seele zu Dir.
Ich war in Dir.
    Ich war ein Teil Deiner Kraft.
Du sandtest Deine Kräfte aus,
    und in der Erde Urbeginn spiegelte sich
    meiner Leibesform erstes Urbild.
In Deinen ausgesandten Kräften
    war ich selbst.
Du warst.
Mein Urbild schaute Dict an.
Es schaute mich selbst an,
    der ich war ein Teil von Dir.
Du warst.

SATURDAY FOR SUNDAY

Great all-encompassing Spirit,
  from Thy life sprang many archetypes,
  long ago when my life-forces
  had yet no present being.
Thou wert.
  I lift up my soul unto Thee.
I was in Thee.
  I was a part of Thy forces.
Thou didst unite Thyself
  at the Earth's first beginning
  with the Life-Sun,
  and gav'st me force of life.
Within Thy radiant life-forces
  was I myself.
Thou wert.
My life-force radiated in Thy force
  into space,
  my body began its becoming,
  within time.
Thou wert.

SAMSTAG FÜR SONNTAG

Grosser umfassender Geist,
  viele Urbilder sprossten aus Deinem Leben,
  damals, als meine Lebenskräfte
  noch nicht vorhanden waren.
Du warst.
  Ich erhebe meine Seele zu Dir.
Ich war in Dir.
  Ich war ein Teil Deiner Kräfte.
Du verbandest Dich
  mit der Erde Urbeginn
  zur Lebenssonne
  und gabest mir die Lebenskraft.
In Deinen strahlenden Lebenskräften
  war ich selbst.
Du warst.
Meine Lebenskraft strahlte in der Deinen
  in den Raum,
  mein Leib begann sein Werden
  in der Zeit.
Du warst.

SUNDAY FOR MONDAY

Great all-encompassing Spirit,
    within Thy forms of life shone forth sensation
    when my sensation
    had yet no present being.
Thou wert.
    I lift up my soul unto Thee.
I was in Thee.
    I was a part of Thy sensations.
Thou didst unite Thyself
    even with the Earth's beginning,
    and in my body began
    the shining forth of own sensation.
Within Thy feelings
    I felt myself.
Thou wert.
My sensations felt Thy Being in themselves.
    My soul began to be within itself,
    since Thou wert in me.
Thou wert.

SONNTAG FÜR MONTAG

Grosser umfassender Geist,
    in Deinen Lebensformen leuchtete Empfindung,
    als meine Empfindung
    noch nicht vorhanden war.
Du warst.
    Ich erhebe meine Seele zu Dir.
Ich war in Dir.
    Ich war ein Teil Deiner Empfindungen.
Du verbandest Dich
    mit der Erde Urbeginn,
    und in meinem Leibe begann
    das Leuchten der eignen Empfindung.
In Deinen Gefühlen
    fühlte ich mich selbst.
Du warst.
Meine Empfindungen fühlten Dein Wesen in sich.
    Meine Seele begann in sich zu sein,
    weil Du in mir warst.
Du warst.

MONDAY FOR TUESDAY

Great encompassing Spirit,
  in Thy sensations lived knowledge,
  when none as yet was given to me.
Thou wert.
  I lift up my soul unto Thee.
I drew into my body.
  In my sensations I lived unto myself.
Thou wert in the Life-Sun;
  in my sensation
  Thy Being lived as my being.
My soul's life
  was outside Thy life.
Thou wert.
My soul felt its own being within.
  In it arose longing—
  the longing for Thee,
  from whom at first it came.
Thou wert.

MONTAG FÜR DIENSTAG

Grosser umfassender Geist,
  in Deinen Empfindungen lebte Erkenntnis,
  als mir noch nicht Erkenntnis gegeben war.
Du warst.
  Ich erhebe meine Seele zu Dir.
Ich zog ein in meinen Leib.
  In meinen Empfindungen lebte ich mir selbst.
Du warst in der Lebenssonne;
  in meiner Empfindung
  lebte Dein Wesen als mein Wesen.
Meiner Seele Leben
  war ausserhalb Deines Lebens.
Du warst.
Meine Seele fühlte ihr eigenes Wesen in sich.
  In ihr erstand Sehnsucht —
  die Sehnsucht nach Dir,
  aus dem sie geworden.
Du warst.

TUESDAY FOR WEDNESDAY

Great all encompassing Spirit,
  In the knowledge of Thy being is world-knowledge,
  Which is to grow mine.
Thou art.
  I will unite my soul with Thee.
May Thine appointed Guide
  enlighten my way.
Feeling Thine appointed Guide
  may I tread the path of life.
He is in the Life-Sun;
  He lived in my longing;
  I will accept His Being
  into mine.
Thou art.
May my strength receive
  the strength of Thine appointed Guide within it.
Blissfulness enters me—
  the bliss wherein the soul discovers Spirit.
Thou art.

DIENSTAG FÜR MITTWOCH

Grosser umfassender Geist,
  in Deines Wesens Erkenntnis ist Welterkenntnis,
  die mir werden soll.
Du bist.
  Ich will einigen meine Seele mit dir.
Dein erkennender Führer
  beleuchte meinen Weg.
Fühlend Deinen Führer
  durchschreite ich die Lebensbahn.
Dein Führer ist in der Lebenssonne;
  er lebte in meiner Sehnsucht;
  aufnehmen will ich sein Wesen in meines.
Du bist.
Meine Kraft nehme auf
  des Führers Kraft in sich.
  Seligkeit zieht in mich—
  die Seligkeit, in der die Seele
  den Geist findet.
Du bist.

WEDNESDAY FOR THURSDAY

Great all-encompassing Spirit,
within Thy Light streams forth life of earth,
my life is in Thine.
Thou art.
My soul is active within Thine.
With Thine appointed Guide I go my way;
I live with Him.
His being is the forming image
of my own being.
Thou art.
Present within my soul the Guide finds Thee,
great all-encompassing Spirit.
Bliss now is mine
from Thy Being's breath.
Thou art.

MITTWOCH FÜR DONNERSTAG

Grosser umfassender Geist,
in Deinem Lichte strahlt der Erde Leben,
mein Leben ist in dem Deinen.
Du bist.
Meine Seele wirkt in der Deinen.
Mit Deinem Führer gehe ich meinen Weg;
ich lebe mit Ihm.
Sein Wesen ist Bild
meines eignen Wesens.
Du bist.
Des Führers Wesen in meiner Seele
findet Dich, umfassender Geist.
Seligkeit wird mir
aus Deines Wesens Hauch.
Du bist.

THURSDAY FOR FRIDAY

Great all-encompassing Spirit,
in Thy Life I live with the life of the earth.
In thee I am.
Thou art.
I am in Thee.
The Guide has brought me to Thee;
I live in Thee.
Thy Spirit is
the forming image of my own being.
Thou art.
Spirit has found
the encompassing Spirit.
Divine Bliss goes onward
to new World-creation.
Thou art. I am. Thou art.

DONNERSTAG FÜR FREITAG

Grosser umfassender Geist,
in Deinem Leben lebe ich mit der Erde Leben.
In Dir bin ich.
Du bist.
Ich bin in Dir.
Der Führer hat mich zu Dir gebracht;
ich lebe in Dir.
Dein Geist ist
meines eignen Wesens Bild.
Du bist.
Gefunden hat Geist
den umfassenden Geist.
Gottseligkeit schreitet
zu neuem Weltschaffen.
Du bist. Ich bin. Du bist.

EVERY DAY, AFTER THE FOREGOING

Great all-encompassing Spirit,
    may my 'I' from below uplift itself on high,
    may it divine Thee in the All-embracing.
May the Spirit of my being glow
    with the light of Thy messengers,
May the Soul of my being be enkindled
    by the fiery flames of thy servers,
The will of my 'I' lay hold
    on the power of Thy Creator-Word.
Thou art.
May Thy *Light* stream into my spirit,
Thy *Life* make warm my soul,
Thy *Being* imbue my will,
so that I win understanding
    for the shining of Thy Light,
    for the loving ardour of Thy Life,
    for Thy Being's Creator-Word.
Thou art.

NACH DEM VORIGEN JEDEN TAG

Grosser umfassender Geist,
    mein Ich erhebe sich von unten nach oben,
    ahnen mög es Dich im Allumfassen.
Der Geist meines Wesens durchleuchte sich
    mit dem Licht Deiner Boten,
Die Seele meines Wesens entzünde sich
    an den Feuerflammen Deiner Diener.
Der Wille meins Ich erfasse
    Deines Schöpferwortes Kraft.
Du bist.
    Dein Licht *strahle in meinen Geist,*
    Dein Leben *erwärme meine Seele,*
    Dein Wesen *durchdringe mein Wollen,*
    dass Verständnis fasse mein Ich
    für Deines Lichtes Leuchten,
    Deines Lebens Liebewärme,
    Deines Wesens Schöpferworte.
Du bist.

Further Mantric Verses

I

Morning

In the spirit lay the germ of my body.
And the spirit has imprinted in my body
The eyes of sense,
That through them I may see
The light of bodies.
And the spirit has imprinted in my body
Reason and sensation
And feeling and will,
That through them I may perceive bodies
And act upon them.
In the spirit lay the germ of my body.

Im Geiste lag der Keim meines Leibes.
Und der Geist hat eingeprägt meinem Leibe
Die sinnliche Augen,
Auf dass ich durch sie sehe
Das Licht der Körper.
Und der Geist hat eingeprägt meinem Leibe
Vernunft und Empfindung
Und Gefühl und Wille
Auf dass ich durch sie wahrnehme die Körper
Und auf sie wirke.
Im Geiste lag der Keim meines Leibes.

Evening

In my body lies the germ of the spirit.
And I will incorporate into my spirit
The supersensuous eyes,
That through them I may behold the light of Spirits.
And I will imprint in my spirit
Wisdom and power and love,
So that through me the spirits may act
And I become the self-conscious organ
Of their deeds.
In my body lies the germ of the spirit.

In meinem Leibe liegt des Geistes Keim.
Und ich will eingliedern meinem Geiste
Die übersinnlichen Augen,
Auf dass ich durch sie schaue das Licht der Geister.
Und ich will einprägen meinem Geiste
Weisheit und Kraft und Liebe,
Auf dass durch mich wirken die Geister
Und ich werde das selbstbewusste Werkzeug
Ihrer Taten.
In Meinem Leibe liegt des Geistes Keim.

II

I look into the Darkness:
In it arises Light,
Living Light.
Who is this Light in the Darkness?
It is I, my real Self.
This reality of the 'I'
Does not enter my earth-existence.
I am only its image.
But I shall find it again
When with good will for the spirit
I have passed through the Gate of Death.

Ich schaue in die Finsternis:
In ihr ersteht Licht,
Lebendes Licht.
Wer ist dies Licht in der Finsternis?
Ich bin es selbst in meiner Wirklichkeit.
Diese Wirklichkeit des Ich
Tritt nicht ein in mein Erdendasein.
Ich bin nur Bild davon.
Ich werde es aber wiederfinden,
Wenn ich,
Guten Willens für den Geist,
Durch des Todes Pforte gegangen.

This meditative verse was given by Rudolf Steiner in London on the evening of 2 September 1923. The lecture leading up to the verse is published with the title: *Man as a Picture of the Living Spirit.* On the morning of the same day the Anthroposophical Society in Great Britain had been founded in the presence of Rudolf Steiner.

III

Spirit of God,
Fill Thou me,
Fill me in my soul.
To my soul give strength,
Strength also to my heart,
My heart that seeks for Thee,
Seeks Thee with earnest longing,
Longing to be whole and well,
Whole and well and full of courage,
Courage the gift from the hand of God,
Gift from Thee, O Spirit of God.
Spirit of God,
Fill Thou me.

O Gottesgeist erfülle mich,
Erfülle mich in meiner Seele;
Meiner Seele leihe starke Kraft,
Starke Kraft auch meinem Herzen,
Meinem Herzen, das dich sucht,
Sucht durch tiefe Sehnsucht,
Tiefe Sehnsucht nach Gesundheit,
Nach Gesundheit und Starkmut
Starkmut der in meine Glieder strömt
Strömt wie edles Gottgeschenk,
Gottgeschenk von dir, o Gottesgeist,
O Gottesgeist erfülle mich.

IV

The soul of the world grows visible
On the cross of the world's body.
In streams of radiance five,
Through wisdom, love and power of will,
Through All-sense and through 'I'-sense
She lives, and finds
Within herself the Spirit of the World.

Es offenbart die Weltenseele sich
Am Kreuze des Weltenleibes.
Sie lebet fünfstrahlig leuchtend,
Durch Weisheit, Liebe, Willenskraft,
Durch Allsinn und durch Ichsinn,
Und findet so
Den Geist der Welt in sich.

V

Bright shines the sun
On the darkness of matter;
So shines with its Light
The whole-making Spirit
On this darkness of soul
In my being a man.
Each time I remember
His glorious power
With genuine warmth
It drenches my weakness
In noonday of Spirit.

Es leuchtet die Sonne
Dem Dunkel des Stoffes;
So leuchtet des Geistes
Allheilendes Wesen
Dem Seelendunkel
In meinem Menschensein.
So oft ich mich besinne
Auf ihre starke Kraft
In rechter Herzenswärme
Durchglänzt sie mich
Mit ihrer Geistesmittagskraft.

VI

I carry Rest within me,
I bear within myself
Forces giving me strength.
Full will I fill myself
With the warmth of these forces,
I will permeate myself
With the power of my will.
And I will feel
How Rest outpours itself
Through all my being,
If I strengthen myself
To come upon Rest
As a force within me
Through this my striving's power.

Ich trage Ruhe in mir,
Ich trage in mir selbst
Die Kräfte, die mich stärken.
Ich will mich erfüllen
Mit dieser Kräfte Wärme,
Ich will mich durchdringen
Mit meines Willens Macht.
Und fühlen will ich
Wie Ruhe sich ergiesst
Durch all mein Sein,
Wenn ich mich stärke,
Die Ruhe als Kraft
In mir zu finden
Durch meines Strebens Macht.

VII

Words of meditation which lay hold of the will

Spirit triumphant
Flame through the weakness
Of faint-hearted souls.
Consume their self-seeking,
Ignite their compassion,
That selfless desire,
The stream through mankind,
May live as a wellspring
Of spirit reborn.

Sieghafter Geist
Durchflamme die Ohnmacht
Zaghafter Seelen.
Verbrenne die Ichsucht,
Entzünde das Mitleid,
Dass Selbstlosigkeit
Der Lebenstrom der Menschheit,
Wallt als Quelle
Der geistigen Wiedergeburt.

For someone who has died

... Let yourself go quiet three times a day, the last time just before dropping off to sleep, so that you take these thoughts with you into the world of the spirit. The best thing is to go to sleep with this in mind:

My love, given in sacrifice,
Shall be woven into the forms
That now envelop you,
Cooling all warmth,
Warming all coldness.
Live supported by love,
Given the gift of light,
As you ascend.

It is important to have the right kind of feeling when you think or say the words 'warmth' and 'coldness'. They do not mean physical 'warmth' or 'coldness', but something like the warmth and coldness we know in our feelings, though it is difficult for someone who is in a physical body to have a real idea of what these qualities mean to someone who is no longer in a body.

Those who have left the body must first of all realize that the astral element which still remains with them continues to be active, though it no longer has its physical instruments. Many things we seek to achieve here on earth are achieved with the aid of those physical instruments. After death they have gone. Not to have physical sense organs is like—but we can only say it is *like*—a feeling of parching thirst in the soul. Those are the powerful 'sensations of heat' experienced once we are disembodied. In the same way our will, formerly used to having physical organs at its disposal which allowed it to achieve its ends, then no longer has those organs. This 'privation' is like a sensation of coldness in the soul.

It is specifically with regard to those sensations that the

living are able to help. These feelings are not merely the outcome of a particular life; they are connected with the mysteries of the incarnation. And because of this it is possible to help those who have left their bodies...

IV
EXPLANATIONS GIVEN IN ESOTERIC CLASSES

Berlin, 24 October 1905

The only summary of the contents of an Esoteric Class written by Rudolf Steiner himself

The verse:

More radiant than the sun,	*Strahlender als die Sonne,*
Purer than the snow,	*Reiner als der Schnee,*
Finer than the ether	*Feiner als der Äther*
Is the Self	*Ist das Selbst,*
The Spirit in my heart.	*Der Geist in meinem Herzen.*
This Self am I,	*Dies Selbst bin Ich,*
I am this Self.	*Ich bin dies Selbst.*

lifts us every morning to our higher Self. Such sayings are not thought out arbitrarily by any particular person, but are drawn from the spiritual world. Much more is therefore contained in them than is ordinarily believed. And one thinks of these in the right way if one assumes that one can never fully fathom their content, but can always find more in them, the more one gives oneself up to them. Hence only indications can ever be given by the Esoteric School as to how one seeks for what they contain. A few such indications are given in what follows.

More radiant than the sun

We see surrounding objects only when they are shone upon by the sun. What makes them visible are the sun's rays thrown back from them into the eye of the beholder. If there were no light, the objects would not be visible. But through this external light only the objects of the physical world become visible. A light 'more radiant than the sun' must illumine man if he is to see things and beings of a soul-spirit nature. This light comes from no outer sun. It proceeds from the fount of light that we kindle in ourselves when we seek within for our higher eternal Self. This higher Self is not of the same origin as our lower self. The latter perceives the everyday environment. But everything that lives in this everyday environment has at some time come into being and will pass away. Hence our experience of it has only a transitory value. And from such perceptions and the thoughts about them our transitory self is built up. All the things which become visible by means of the sun were at one time not in existence and someday they will no longer be there. The sun, too, once came into being and will at some time pass away. But the soul exists for the very purpose of recognizing the eternal in things. When some-day the whole earth will be no more, the souls who inhabited it will still exist. And what these souls have experienced on earth will be borne by them somewhere else as a memory.

If a person has done me a kindness, the deed passes away. But what the deed has planted in my soul, that remains. And the bond of love that has thus united me with him does not pass away. Whatever we experience is always the source in us of something that endures. We ourselves thus draw the enduring out of things and carry it over into eternity. And when someday human beings are transplanted to a quite different scene of action, they will bring with them what they have gathered here. And their deeds in the new world will be woven out of the memories of the old. For there is no seed that does not bear fruit.

If we are united with somebody by love, then this love is a seed, and we experience its fruit all through the future, since we belong together with such a person throughout the future. Thus there lives in us something which is inter-woven with the divine power that binds all things together into the eternal fabric of the universe. This 'something' is our higher Self. And *this* is 'more radiant than the sun'. The light of the sun illumines a person only from outside. His

Soul Sun illumines him from within. Hence it is more radiant than the sun.

Purer than the snow

In itself everything is pure. It can become impure only when it unites with something that should not be united with it. Water in itself is pure. But even the dirt in dirty water would be pure if it were by itself, if it had not wrongfully united with water. Carbon by itself is pure. It becomes dirt only if it is wrongfully united with water. Now when water assumes its own form in the snow crystal, it separates out all that has united wrongly with it. So does the human soul become pure if it separates out all that should not be united with it. And to the soul belongs the divine, the imperishable. Every ideal, every thought of something great and beautiful, belongs to the inner form of the soul. And when it meditates upon such ideals, such thoughts, then it purifies itself, as the water purifies itself in becoming snow crystal. And since the spiritual is purer than anything material, so the 'higher Self', the soul which lives in the heights, is 'purer than the snow'.

Finer than the ether

Ether is the finest material. But all that is material is still dense in relation to the element of soul. It is not the dense which is enduring, but the 'fine'. The stone we think of as solid will pass away. But the thought of the stone, which lives in the soul, remains. God has thought this thought. And out of it He made the dense stone. As ice is only densified water, so is the stone only a densified thought of God's. All objects are such densified thoughts of God. The 'higher Self', however, dissolves all things, and within it live God's thoughts. And when the Self is woven of such God-thoughts, then it is 'finer than the ether'.

The Spirit in my heart

Man has understood something only when he has grasped it with his heart. Intellect and reason are merely media for this understanding by the heart. Through intellect and reason we penetrate to the divine thoughts. But when we have thus reached the thought, we must learn to *love* it. Man learns little by little to love all things. This does not mean that he should give his heart without discrimination to everything he encounters. For experience is at first deceptive. But if one takes pains to fathom a being or an object down to its divine foundation, then one also begins to love it.

If a depraved human being confronts me, I should in no way love his depravity. In that case I should only be in error and I should not be helping him. If, however, I ponder over how this person has arrived at his depraved state, and if I help him to give it up, then I help him and I myself struggle through to truth. I must search everywhere as to *how* I can love. God is in all things, but the divinity is something I must first search for. I am not straightaway to love that external aspect of a being or a thing, for this is deceptive and I could then easily love his error. But behind all illusion lies truth, and truth one can always love. And if the heart seeks the love of truth in all beings, then there lives the 'Spirit in the heart'. Such love is the garment that the soul should ever wear. Then the soul itself weaves the divine into things.

* * *

The members of the School should use many free minutes of the day in linking such thoughts to the divine maxims of wisdom. They should never think they have completely understood such a maxim, but always assume that still more lies in it than they have already found. Through such an attitude one comes to feel that in all genuine wisdom lies the key to the infinite, and in this feeling one binds oneself to the infinite.

* * *

It is not a matter of meditating on many sentences, but of letting a little live again and again in the quietened soul.

During the meditation one should seldom speculate, but peacefully let the content of the sentences work upon one. But apart from the meditation, one should return in free moments to the content of the sentences and see what reflections one can draw from them. Then they become a living power which sinks into the soul and makes it strong and vigorous. For when the soul unites with eternal truth, it lives in the Eternal. And when the soul lives in the Eternal, then the Higher Beings have access to it and can let their own power sink into it.

Concerning the Union of the Image
with the Archetype

Berlin, Good Friday, 13 April 1906

The Aum and the Easter Thought

Everything physical around us arises and passes away; only the Archetypes of things do not arise and pass away. They are not created nor do they pass away; they are eternal. The physical earth arises and passes away, but the Archetype of the earth does not arise or pass away. The Archetype of the earth is eternal. And within the Archetype of the earth all other Archetypes of the physical world are contained. Like that of the earth they do not arise nor do they pass away; they are eternal. As the earth has its eternal Archetype, so every mineral, every plant, every animal has its own, which radiates through eternity in beauty and splendour.

Man must learn to unite himself more and more closely with the Archetypes of things. He must climb upwards to them. He learns to unite himself with them through acts of recollection. When in the evening the pupil looks in backward order over the day that is spent, recalling the scenes of the day, the pleasures and sorrows he has experienced, when he lets the pleasures and sorrows that were associated with the day's events pass again through his soul in remembrance, he places himself in connection with the life that endures and is still present even without the material reality. Through his power of imagining he must recall the events in his own life and in the lives of others, and must let the joy and sorrow that were associated with the events flow through his soul. Thereby he learns how to ascend to the Beings who embody themselves in joy and sorrow, and he learns to live consciously in the soul-world. We are surrounded all the time by these spiritual Beings. Then we learn to perceive them.

When we endeavour to call up into remembrance experiences in which we ourselves were directly involved, this is different from thinking back to events of which we have read or heard. The difference is that in the former case our own *Self* was present. And that is the essential point. It is good to train ourselves to call back into remembrance experiences from our own past. A pain, a joy we once felt, looks quite different in remembrance from what it was at the time. Through such acts of recollection we approach true knowledge. We see things as they really are if we can reach the stage of actually feeling a pain or a joy which is not ours. If we are capable of causing images of things we no longer see to rise up in us, we thereby draw nearer to the creative Godhead.

In Rosicrucian Schools, such teachings were given to the pupils. Out of their own volition they had to let pass through their souls the pleasure and displeasure which were associated with former events in life, now without their brutal reality. If pleasure and displeasure are allowed to rise up in the soul in this way, the organs of soul are awakened. For a pupil who was not yet capable of bringing this about himself, dramatic pictures, scenes from human life, were presented by initiates for the purpose of awakening these organs in him. By witnessing them a man learnt to feel, without its brutal reality, what is normally bound up with the events themselves. That is what remains of events in the world. Man must learn to rise to this level.

Man will remember former lives on earth in so far as he has learnt to know the Eternal in things, and in so far as he himself brings something eternal into the world.

The yoga pupil performs breathing exercises. Ordinary breathing is irregular, without rhythm. The yoga pupil learns to bring rhythm into his breathing. Unrhythmic breathing is really a process of killing; through the breath streaming out from him, man kills. He brings death to himself and to other living beings so long as the breath has not become rhythmic and full of life through yoga training. Through rhythmic breathing, also, human breathing becomes individual. With savages, even their actions are scarcely individual. The higher a man ascends in evolution, the more will his action bear an individual stamp. To begin with, all breathing is alike even among highly evolved human beings; now man must learn to individualize his breathing. By this use of breathing he works his own unique being more and more into the surrounding world. As much of himself as he works into the surrounding world through his breathing, so much remains behind as eternal, imperishable, and so much of himself will he find again in all subsequent incarnations. He transforms the world around him through a rhythmical breathing process and in this way is a co-worker in cosmic events. He works creatively upon the earth itself.

Whereas the breathing of the ordinary man kills, the breathing of a purified man brings life to the surrounding world. The air in the towns is bad not only because it is polluted by all kinds of physical elements, but also because it is corrupted by the unrhythmic, unpurified breathing of man. The air in towns is full of poisons derived from the immorality of man. In the country the air is purer than in the towns. Human beings there still lead a simpler, more rhythmical life, in greater tranquillity. Whereas in the towns man is filled with thoughts of thousands of things which flood through his life unrhythmically, in the country man is accustomed to fit his life into the rhythmical course of nature, into the rhythms of growth and withering, into the rhythm of the seasons of the year. Every year, in rhythmic harmony with nature, he sets about definite tasks at different times, and thereby places himself in a far more intimate connection with the great cosmic laws than does the town-dweller, who pays no heed whatever to these laws. By thus merging himself rhythmically into the course of cosmic life, the country dweller brings rhythm also into his own life. Through such rhythm, the very air he expires becomes more rhythmical, purer, better. The plants stream out pure air. They are chaste, without greed, selfless; that is why man feels well amid the plant world. It streams out life. But the ordinary man brings death to the surrounding world with his breathing. Through a pure, moral, selfless way of living he must transform his breathing into breathing that is pure and full of life, and through yoga exercises he must bring rhythm into it. Then he must learn to pour out his individuality into his breathing, imprinting it into the world. Thereby he gives life to the surrounding world. Through continued training of this kind, the yogi learns to hover over the purely physical, to transport himself into the Eternal. He thereby ascends to the eternal, imperishable Archetypes of things that neither arise nor pass away; he also unites himself with his own Archetype. Man comes into existence and passes out of existence, in the physical sense. But for every human being there is an Archetype—an Archetype that is eternal.

If the yogi learns to unite himself with the Archetypes, then he has ascended to the eternal world of the spirit. He hovers above the transitory. That is the condition of which it is said that the yogi then rests between the Wings of the Great Bird, the Swan, the AUM.

The AUM is the way back from the images of the Archetype—the ascent into the Eternal. This ascent into the Eternal, the union of the Self with the Archetypes, is also expressed in the mantra from the Upanishads:

Yasmāj jātam jagat sarvam, yasminn eva praliyate
yenedam dhriyate caiva, tasmai jñānātmane namah.

This is what lies also in the Easter Thought. It is the resurrection of man from attachment to the transitory and material into the eternal regions of the Archetypes. Nature serves as a symbol for this. As at the time of Easter new life springs up everywhere from the earth, after the seed-germ has first sacrificed itself and decayed in the earth to enable new life to arise, so too must all the lower nature in man die away. He must sacrifice the lower nature in order that he may rise to the eternal Archetypes of things. That is why Christendom, too, at this time when nature awakens from winter sleep, celebrates the Death and the Resurrection of the Redeemer.

Man, too, must first die, in order then to experience the resurrection in the spirit. Only he who overcomes attachment to the transitory can himself become eternal like the eternal Archetypes, only he can rest between the Wings of the Great Bird, the AUM. Then he becomes one of those who co-operate in the world's progress. Then he helps to fashion it for a future existence; then, from out of his inmost being, he works into the world with magic power.

Archetypal Self, from which we have proceeded,
Archetypal Self, who lives with all things,
To thee, thou higher Self, we return again.

Urselbst, von dem wir ausgegangen sind,
Urselbst, welches in allen Dingen lebt,
Zu dir, du höheres Selbst, kehren wir zurück.

Building up the Spiritual Body
through Meditation

Berlin, 2 October 1906

In a humble and modest way we should feel gratified that we have been deemed worthy of taking part in the Esoteric School. It is not by chance that we arrived at this point. The fact that we sought it and were granted access to it should prove to us that we have already been striving in this direction over several lifetimes. The outer world can no longer fulfil us; we cannot be wholly absorbed by it. If we could have been we would not have sought the path that led us here. The outer world represents the full flourishing of the Fifth Root Race; alongside this flourishing, the morning light of the Sixth Day, or the Sixth Root Race, is already dawning. This will be a far more spiritual one; the spiritual body will become far more developed. It will be the first flowering of what will come to full fruition in the Sixth Root Race.We who take part in the Esoteric School belong to the dawning light of the Sixth Day; we follow and serve the great Master who guides its progress. Our task is to create and give birth to this spiritual body out of ourselves. Our physical body is not our 'I'; we should not identify ourselves with it. We received it in the solid mineral form in which it now is, as a tool for accomplishing the tasks of the Fifth Root Race. We must form and take hold of it as a tool; our 'I' should be master of it. In earlier times our 'I' had a differently formed tool. The body of the Fourth Root Race, the Atlantean, had not yet experienced the separation of sun and rain; it moved through undulating mists. It was in many respects differently constituted — yet our 'I' was the same. Even more different were the bodies of the Lemurian race, particularly in the initial stages; they floated and hovered in a watery, airy element. The same 'I' was working upon them. Our physical body is born of the macrocosm. The outer world formed it; out of our physical body our 'I' must give birth to the spiritual body. Our spiritual body is named 'Atma'. Atma means 'breath'. By means of regulated breathing in meditation, we build up our spiritual body. We really breathe our 'I' in and out with every breath.

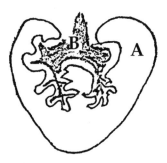

A. Physical organs, physical body, etheric body, astral body
B. Manas, Buddhi, Atma (spirit-self...)

This drawing can help us to understand what actually happens. Within our outer body, which the Gods have built up, we form our spiritual body. The 'I' streams into it with every in-breath and out again when we breathe out. When we regulate our breathing and concentrate it in various parts of our body, we provide our spiritual body with the forces that are necessary to build it up. The 'I' is in direct connection with the point of the forehead slightly above and behind the nose; thinking is connected with the larynx, feeling with the hands, willing with the feet and the whole lower frame of the body. If we let these forces stream through our body with the help of regulated breathing, we build up our spiritual body.

In the Spirit lay the germ of my body...
(see page 70)

Notes taken from the same lesson by someone else

During the course of his inner development, specific exercises are given to the pupil, by means of which he should build up his spirit-self. With instruction from his teacher he should undertake breathing exercises. These exist in order to help spiritualize him. The human being has an organ that fills with air when be breathes in, and empties of air when he breathes out.

When he breathes in, the air enters into the most delicate passages of this organ. This organ is the lung. The spirit of the human being lives in the air. When he inhales, he breathes his spirit in; when he exhales, he breathes it out. The spirit of the human being is continually evolving. It is, at one moment, within him, the next moment outside him in the world. Through breathing in and out, the development of the spirit-self is nurtured.

It is very important what the human being conveys to his spirit as he breathes out. He builds up his spirit through his thoughts. He builds it up with every thought that passes into the breath he exhales. The human being did not always have an organ for breathing air. If we look back at previous planetary stages, at the Moon, we find beings that inhaled fire, not air. Just as the human being now breathes in oxygen and breathes out carbon dioxide, so the beings of that time breathed in warmth and breathed out coldness.

A time will come when the human being no longer breathes air. In the same way that he now engenders his own warmth through the organ of warmth, through the heart and the circulation of blood — whereas once the beings on the Moon sucked and breathed in warmth — so one day he will have an inner organ of air providing the organism with what it at present takes from the outer air. In the future, human beings will be able to assimilate the used air within themselves. When that has been achieved they will no longer take in air from their environment, they will not live in the air. In a later stage, on Jupiter, human beings will live in light and breathe light, as they now breathe air and as they breathed warmth on the Moon.

There will also come a time, still on this earth, when the human being will live only in his spirit, using his body only as a tool; this time is already approaching. It is true that we live in the Fifth Day of mankind, in the Fifth Race and evolutionary period of our earth. But in the spiritual world the Sixth Dawn is already breaking. Mankind already lives there in the Dawn of the Sixth Day.

The Awakening of Man to
Self-consciousness

Berlin, 14 November 1906

In these studies, the exercises which those engaged in occult training have to carry out will be explained more closely. For one who is not practising these exercises, the explanations should be a preparation for the time when he too will have to carry them out. The great Masters of Wisdom and of the Harmony of Feelings guide us in our inner striving for knowledge.

An exercise known to many is this: one first concentrates on the point at the root of the nose, between the eyebrows, in the inner part of the head; then on the point in the interior of the larynx; then on the point, extended into a line, which stretches from the shoulders into the arms and hands; then on the more widely extended point which spreads over the whole surface of the body. In the secret knowledge, these lines and surfaces are also spoken of as points. We will now learn to understand this exercise more fully.

For this, we must go far back in thought, to the Lemurian epoch. The earth's appearance was then altogether different. The rocks that are now solid then flowed like water. Air in the modern sense did not yet exist; the whole earth was enveloped in hot vapours. Many metals which are solid today were present then in gaseous form or flowed like water; the vaporous atmosphere was pervaded by currents of ether, as is the present-day atmosphere by currents of air. Man already lived on this earth. But he was a creature half fish, half bird, hovering or swimming as he moved along. At that time an important event took place in the process of human evolution — man developed a skin and thereby shut himself off from the rest of the world as an independent being. Until then he had not been separate from his environment; the streaming currents of the whole world penetrated into him. Now he shut himself off behind his skin. The process of separation from the environment was brought about by a particular ether-stream.

After a certain time there was a further significant event. Man assumed the upright posture, thereby giving a definite direction to his whole striving and development. Before that time the position of his body was like that of the animal today. Only now could he develop his forelimbs into arms and hands as they now are, i.e. fit for work in the real sense. Only now did he begin to work as an independent being; only now was it possible for him to develop individual karma. No animal can do this. Only a being who walks and stands upright creates individual karma. A second, definite ether-stream brought about this transformation.

A third ether-stream resulted in a third important transformation. Only when man had assumed an upright posture could lungs develop in the form to be found only in man, and in connection with them the larynx formed itself out of delicate etheric substances. The gradual development of human speech was now possible.

Through a fourth ether-stream the organ lying between the eyebrows at the root of the rose was formed, and thereby man awoke for the first time to self-consciousness — to *consciousness* of self. Before then he had only a *feeling* of self.

If now one directs the attention firmly and forcefully to one — always one at a time — of these four points, the root of the nose, the larynx, the hands and arms, the whole bodily surface, combining with this exercise a particular word (which can be imparted only verbally, from teacher to pupil), then one enters into connection with the corresponding ether-stream which called forth the transformation in the human body. Occult training consists paramountly in this, that we become conscious of the processes that work below the level of consciousness on our body. We have to enter into conscious connection with the forces of the cosmos.

If the hands are crossed so that the right hand lies over the left, and one concentrates on the hands thus crossed in connection with a particular word, then, provided the exercise is performed often enough with the greatest possible energy and persistence, one will soon notice that the two hands strive apart and the arms spread out quite of themselves. It is the posture of the medieval saints.

This exercise, too, has its definite significance. Streams of ether are always circulating out of the cosmos through the human body. One such stream enters through the head, passes from there into the right foot, then into the left hand, then into the right hand, then into the left foot, and from there back to the head. If we think of a man standing in the position just described, with outstretched arms, then the streaming has the form of a pentagram. It would be bad for man if the stream did not enter into him through the head but through the feet. All evil influences enter the human body through the feet. The black magicians make use of this. This stream, however, circulates in man not only when he finds himself in this particular position but also whenever the hands are superimposed, or one leg is bent. There are five different ether vibrations through the human body. One of them also circulates in solid substance and is therefore called 'earthy', because it can permeate the solid earth as well.

These streams circulate all the time in man and bring him into connection with the entire cosmos.

The being of man is woven out of the spirit, we are born from out of the spirit, we have descended into matter, and flow back again to the spirit. The streams which were active in us during our descent into matter should now become conscious to us. We go back along the same path by which we have come, but consciously. There is no other true evolution. What we now kindle in ourselves through these exercises will be developed by humanity at large only in the Sixth Root Race. In spiritual science, a Root Race is called a Day of Creation. We are at the point where the Sixth Day of Creation is being prepared; we are in the dawn of the Sixth Day of Creation. The descent from the spirit, the life in matter and the return to the spirit are presented in three letters:

AUM...

The Foundations of Esoteric Training

Munich, 6 June 1907

We must be clear what the proper foundations are for an esoteric training and what its true nature consists of. The school to which we belong is composed of different circles. All those who have newly joined it are the 'seekers'. Those who make some progress belong to the 'practising' students, and after this stage follows the actual 'training'. Our school is composed of these three groups. We all entered the Esoteric School in order to develop certain organs within us, which can enable us to experience the higher worlds for ourselves. How does one develop organs within oneself? All our organs have been built up as a result of our own previous activity. Let us take an example to clarify this. There was once a time when none of us yet had eyes. At that time, the human being floated and swam in a watery primeval sea. He had an organ for orientating himself, which is now only present in a vestigial form. This is the so-called pineal gland, which lies in the upper part of the middle of the head, and is somewhat involuted. We can see it in some animals if we remove the top of the skull. This organ enabled the primeval human being to perceive whether he was approaching something helpful or harmful. Above all, though, it was an organ for perceiving warmth and cold. When, in those times, the sun shone down upon the earth, the human being could not see it; but the pineal gland led him to the parts of the watery ocean which it had warmed. And this warmth gave him a feeling of great delight. He would remain there for long periods, drawing very close to the surface so that the rays of the sun could warm him. And because the sun's rays fell directly upon his body, the eyes began to be formed. Two things, therefore, were necessary for eyes to develop: the sun had to shine, firstly, but the human beings also had to swim to the sun-warmed places and expose themselves to the sun. If they had not done that, but instead had said, 'I will only develop what is already in me,' then they might well have developed a larger and larger pineal gland — a monster of an organ — but they would never have received eyes.

We must think in this same way about the development of spiritual eyes. One should not say: 'The higher worlds are already within me, I only need to develop and draw them out.' The primeval people were not able to draw the sun out of themselves, but they could form the organs with which they could see it. We also can only form the organs to see the spiritual sun and the higher worlds; we cannot draw them out of ourselves. And we will never be able to develop these organs if, on the one hand, we do not hurry to expose ourselves to it so that it can. The places where the spiritual sun shines for us are the esoteric schools; all those who feel drawn to the esoteric schools are warmed by its rays when they heed the instructions and directions they receive there. Every organ which had a past will also have a future. The pineal gland will, in the future, again become an important organ. Those who are in the esoteric schools are already working at its formation. The exercises which we receive affect not only the astral and etheric bodies but also the pineal gland. When their effect becomes very penetrating, it permeates from the pineal gland into the lymph vessels and from there into the blood. All human beings will, in the future, have a developed pineal gland — not only those who now practise occult exercises. But in the case of those who constitute the evil race, it will be an organ for the worst and most terrible impulses, and so big that the greatest part of the body will consist of it. Just as one sees a host of midges in the distance as a swarm, so, if one looked down from space at the earth when the host of glandular human bodies are wandering about on it, one would see the earth itself as a great gland. But those who form their pineal gland in the right way will have a very precious and perfect organ. Now we are going to examine more closely the exercises which are given to us, remembering that they are ones which render our souls receptive to the spiritual sun-rays. The six subsidiary exercises serve as a preparation for the actual occult exercises. Whoever dedicates himself to them with proper seriousness and enthusiasm will find that they develop in him the fundamental disposition of soul which is necessary to reap the benefit of the occult exercises.

1. *Control of one's thoughts.* We should find at least five free minutes every day and contemplate a thought which is as insignificant as possible, which does not hold any interest for us whatsoever. Everything which we can possibly think about the topic should be logically ordered and arranged. It is important that it should not be a significant or very interesting theme, for it is precisely the self-discipline we need to concentrate on it for a long time which can awaken the slumbering faculties of the soul. After some time one will notice a feeling of stability and certainty in the soul. We must not imagine, though, that this feeling will suddenly and powerfully come over us. No, it is a very subtle and delicate feeling which we must carefully listen out for. Those who will say that they could find absolutely no trace of this feeling are like somebody who goes out to find a tiny delicate object from among many other objects. He searches, it is true, but only generally and superficially, overlooking the tiny object. We must grow very still and listen inwardly, then we will find this feeling; we will become aware of it in the front part of the head. When we sense it there, we should picture it flowing into the brain and then into the spinal cord. Gradually we will then have the feeling that rays are streaming from the forehead down into the spinal column.

2. *Initiative in one's actions.* For this one must choose an action which one thinks of oneself. If someone was to try to exercise his initiative by adopting the activity of watering a flower, which is the example given in the relevant instructions, he would be doing something quite pointless. For the action must spring from our own initiative, one must have thought of it oneself. After practising this exercise for a while we will soon have a feeling which could be expressed as: 'I can achieve something', 'I can do more than previously', 'I wish to be active'. One actually feels this in the whole upper part of the body. We then try to let this feeling flow towards the heart.

3. *Mastering joy and sorrow.* We may feel sometimes an urge to cry. Then it is time to practise this exercise. We force ourselves with all our strength not to cry for once. The same with laughing. We try, on some occasion when we feel laughter rising up, not to laugh but to remain peaceful. That does not mean that we should not laugh any more; but we should be able to take hold of ourselves, be master over laughing and crying. When we have overcome ourselves in this way a few times, we will have a feeling of peace and equanimity. We allow this feeling to flow through the whole body, pouring it out from the heart first of all into the arms and hands, so that it can radiate out from the hands into our actions. Then we let it stream down to the feet and last of all up to the head. This exercise requires earnest self-observation and should take at least a quarter of an hour each day.

4. *Positivity.* We should know how to find the grain of goodness and beauty in everything bad and ugly, and we should also be able to perceive in every criminal the spark of godliness. Then we feel that we are spreading out beyond our skin. It is a similar feeling of enlargement to that which the etheric body has after death. When we sense this feeling we should let it radiate out of ourselves

through the eyes, ears and the whole skin, but particularly through the eyes.

5. *Lack of prejudice.* We should remain flexible, always capable of taking in new information. If someone relates something to us which we think sounds improbable, we must nevertheless always keep a tiny corner of our heart open, in which we say: 'He could be right after all.' This does not need to make us completely uncritical, for we can always examine and test such statements. When we practise this, a feeling comes over us as if something was streaming into us from outside. We draw this in through the eyes, ears and the whole skin.

6. *Equilibrium.* The five precious feelings should now be harmonized with each other by taking notice of them all simultaneously.

These exercises do not have to take exactly one month each. Some indication of time had to be given. What is important, though, is that one practises them in the particular order given here. If anyone should practise the second exercise before the first, he would derive absolutely no benefit from it. The order is very important. Some people even believe that they ought to begin with the sixth exercise, the harmonizing one. But nothing can be harmonized which is not already there. Whoever does not practise the exercises in the given order will gain nothing at all from them. To begin with the sixth exercise is as senseless as if one needed to take six steps to cross a bridge and tried to take the sixth step first.

Most of us have also received a morning meditation. One should do this early in the morning at a time one has decided for oneself, which one keeps to as strictly as possible. First of all one concentrates deeply upon seven lines. For some of us these are as follows:

In purest outpoured light
Shimmers the Godhead of the world.
In purest love towards all that is
Outpours the godhood of my soul.
I rest within the Godhead of the world;
There shall I find myself,
Within the Godhead of the world.

During meditation one should not speculate about these seven lines, but live wholly within them. One should picture them vividly to oneself.

In purest outpoured light

Here one feels the pouring beams of the light flooding around one, permeating one from all sides; one imagines its radiance as clearly as possible.

Shimmers the Godhead of the world

One imagines that it is God who streams into one in these rays; one seeks to feel Him and to take Him up into oneself.

In purest love towards all that is
Outpours the godhood of my soul.

One imagines that one is radiating out the godly beams which one took into oneself, pouring them out for the good of all beings.

The last lines should awaken the idea and feeling that one is wholly embedded in the divine rays and that one finds oneself within them. Whoever wishes to imagine this in a particularly tangible form can also, finally, imagine a tree which he loves, which he likes returning to.

After these seven lines we each have a word or a phrase in which we should become absorbed. This concentration on a word or phrase, for example 'Strength', is very important. It is a kind of mantra or word of power, which is precisely suited to the state of soul of each individual. One should let this word resound in the soul in a similar way to striking a tuning fork. Just as one listens to the fading tone of the tuning fork, so one should let the word quietly fade in the soul after one has concentrated on it, should give oneself over to the effect this word has had in our soul.

Finally one concentrates deeply for five minutes on one's own divine ideal. The precise nature of this ideal does not matter, it is just a question of creating the right mood of soul. It does not matter whether one thinks of one's teacher or of the starry heavens. Atheists, who said they had no divine ideal, have before now allowed themselves to think of the starry heavens in this regard, for no one can avoid feeling awe and reverence towards them.

Whoever begins these exercises should keep doing them and not give them up when he feels like it. The astral and etheric bodies soon get used to them and will revolt if they do not receive them. An interruption or a complete cessation of these exercises is certainly very dangerous.

The *evening review of the day* is also important. It must be undertaken backwards, from the end of the day to the beginning, since we ought to accustom ourselves to the mode of perception of the astral plane. During this review one should visualize everything as vividly as possible. To begin with, of course, if one has 80 important experiences to review, one cannot visualize each one of them vividly. One must then choose a considered selection, until the whole day unfurls before one like a tableau. Once again, it is the little insignificant occurrences which matter, for what awakens the powers of the soul is the effort which one makes.

The Importance of the Year 1879

Commentary on a Meditation
Berlin, 9 October 1907

Everything that is spoken in an esoteric lesson is brought to us directly from the Masters, and he who utters it is only an instrument of their intentions.

The difference between an exoteric and an esoteric lecture consists in this: in the former, teaching, knowledge, are received; in the latter, something is *experienced*. The Masters speak continually to men. Only those who are prepared, those whose souls are opened in such a way that the Masters can find access to them, can hear their voices. Esoteric work is of the utmost importance for the evolution of the cosmos — yet also for those in the humblest social position.

The year 1879 marks an epoch of the greatest significance in the evolution of humanity because of an event which took place on the astral plane; since then our civilization has taken a different direction.

A certain spiritual stream began to flow in the year 1250 and reached its height in 1459, when Christian Rosenkreutz was raised to the rank of Knight of the Rose Cross. In 1510 began the Age known in occultism as the Age of *Gabriel.* The Age of *Michael* began in 1879; after that comes the Age of *Oriphiel,* when great conflicts will rage among men; therefore a tiny handful are now being prepared to keep the torch of spiritual knowledge alight in that sombre epoch.

Commentary on the Meditation, 'In purest outpoured Light'

(See page 31.) Imaginative presentation of the single strophes:

In purest outpoured Light
Shimmers the Godhead of the world

The Godhead pours Himself out as it were in silver-shining moonlight over the outer world: we feel as if this light is streaming through us, flowing around us.

In purest Love towards all that is
Outpours the godhood of my soul

After expanding into the outer world, where we sought to know the Godhead, we sink deeply within our own being, and through the love which unites us with all beings we find the link with the Godhead and feel the divine element in our own soul.

I rest within the Godhead of the world.

The word *Ruhe* has magic power. The pupil who succeeds in concentrating himself in it and letting it act upon him feels as if he were bathed and pervaded by rest and peace. In that we feel within ourselves the connection with the Godhead, we find this rest and this peace within us: rest encircles us, penetrates into us.

There shall I find myself,
Within the Godhead of the world...

And now there arises in us an image of a point of light, a gleaming spark shimmering towards us from afar and to which we strive ... and wherein we shall find ourselves in the bosom of the Godhead.

Concerning the Breathing Process

Munich, 16 January 1908

In our last esoteric lesson we were preoccupied with the great laws and principles of spiritual life which reveal themselves throughout human evolution; with the great spiritual powers which oversee everything occurring on the physical plane and which assume leadership from one another through cycles of time. In contrast to this, I would like today to discuss laws of spiritual life in a somewhat more intimate way, by examining the inner life of the human being.

Whoever embarks on an occult training is a seeker who must, in some respects, wait. He waits with the expectation that some day a new world will be revealed to him, different from the one he normally perceives. He waits with the expectation that one day he will be able to say: 'I perceive a new world. Amidst all the things which I previously perceived in physical space, I now see spiritual beings in abundance, who before were hidden from me.' For you to understand this clearly, you must recollect the seven stages of consciousness which the human being passes through in the course of his evolution. The first of these was a dull, dim level of consciousness, in which the human being felt himself one with the cosmos; we call this condition the Saturn stage. In the Sun stage, consciousness encompassed less but was correspondingly brighter. As the human being passed through Moon existence, his consciousness was similar to what we experience, in its last vestiges, in our dreams—a dull picture-consciousness. In our present stage upon earth we have a bright day-consciousness; this will remain with us when, on Jupiter, we again develop a picture-consciousness, but it will then be an illumined picture-consciousness. The human being will subsequently ascend to two further stages: to inspiration- and intuitive-consciousness. Our bright day-consciousness therefore stands at the midpoint between the dull picture-consciousness of the Moon stage and the illumined picture-consciousness of Jupiter. The esoteric student waits for the Jupiter-consciousness to be, some day, revealed to him. Every one of you will attain this—some sooner, others later (this depends on the capacities of each one, on the degree of his inner readiness).

Every human being carries within himself the seeds of Jupiter-consciousness. This future consciousness manifests in a very delicate, tentative way, which the human being is not able to recognize. Esoteric life consists to a large extent in learning to interpret correctly the subtle processes in oneself and in one's environment. The old Moon-consciousness, also, has not completely vanished; the last vestiges of it remain. Both the old Moon-consciousness and the new Jupiter-consciousness are to be found in the human being of today—the former in feelings of shame, the latter in feelings of fear and anxiety. In feelings of shame, in which the blood is pushed up towards the surface of the body, to its periphery, there live the last vestiges of Moon-consciousness. In feelings of anxiety, in which the blood flows back towards the heart, the Jupiter-consciousness announces itself. Our normal day-consciousness branches out in these two directions.

When we feel shame about something and blush, we experience something which is a recollection of Moon-existence. Imagine a Moon-person. He was not yet able to say 'I' to himself, but lived in a dim, dull picture-consciousness, completely embedded in astral powers and beings with whom he felt himself united and in harmony. Imagine, my brothers and sisters, that suddenly, one day, such a Moon-person began to feel: 'I am an "I". I am different from the others, I am an independent being and all the other beings in my environment are looking at me.' The shame such a Moon-person would have felt, would have burned in him overpoweringly; he would have tried to vanish, to die from shame, if he had experienced such a premature 'I'-feeling. When we feel shame, my sisters and brothers, we also would like to vanish, sink under the floorboards, dissolve our 'I'. Imagine how the old Moon-person was embedded in a harmony with the powers and beings of his environment. If another being approached him in enmity, he did not need to consider what to do; he knew instinctively how to avoid it. He acted in a way that, if he had been conscious, he would roughly have expressed as follows: 'I know that the world's laws do not allow for this wild animal to tear me to pieces; the world's harmony is such that there must be means to protect myself from my enemy.' The old Moon-person felt himself in complete harmony with the powers of the universe. If an 'I'-feeling had awoken in him, this harmony would have been instantly disturbed. And, in fact, as the 'I'-feeling began to permeate the human being on earth, it brought him increasingly into disharmony with his environment. Whoever has supersensible hearing hears the universe resounding in a mighty harmony; when he compares this with the tones reaching him from individual human beings, he hears a discord—greater in some cases, less in others, but still a discord. It is your task to resolve and dissolve this discord into harmony through your continued evolution. This discord has arisen through the 'I'; yet it came about through the wisdom of the spiritual powers which rule and guide the universe. If human beings had remained in harmony, they would never have come to independence. Discord was introduced so that the human being could freely regain harmony out of his own strength. For this reason it was necessary that the 'I'-feeling, conscious of itself, should develop at the cost of inner harmony. When the time comes for the Jupiter-consciousness to be kindled and the human being regains a harmonious relationship with the powers of the cosmos, then he will preserve his self-aware 'I'-feeling in his new condition of consciousness; he will be an independent 'I' and yet will also be in harmony with the universe.

We have seen that the new Jupiter-consciousness is already announcing itself in the capacity for fear and anxiety. But it is always so that when a future condition appears too early it is premature and out of place. You can understand this through an example. A flower which should bloom in August can be 'forced' in a hothouse so that it flowers already in May. In August, the time of its proper flowering, no further blossom can unfold; its strength is exhausted and it can no longer find its right place within the conditions to which it belongs. In May, also, it will die the moment it is taken out of the hothouse, since it does not belong in the context of that season. It is the same with feelings of anxiety. They have no place today, and will have one still less in the future. What occurs when we feel anxious? The blood is driven back into the centre of the human being, into the heart, in order to form a firm central point and make the human being strong in opposition to the outer world. It is the inmost power of the 'I' which does this. This power of the 'I', which affects the blood, must become ever stronger and more conscious; on Jupiter the human being will then be able to direct the blood to his central point quite consciously, so as to make himself strong. What is harmful and unnatural today, however, is the feeling of fear which is connected with this flow of the blood. In the future that must no longer be so; only the powers of the 'I', without any fear, must be active.

Throughout human evolution, the outer world becomes ever more antagonistic towards us. You must continually, increasingly, to set your inner strength against this outer world that presses upon you. But anxiety must vanish. It is especially necessary for anyone who proceeds with an esoteric training to free himself from all feelings of fear and anxiety. Anxiety only has a certain justification in making us aware that we need to make ourselves strong, but all unnatural feelings of anxiety which torment the human being must disappear altogether. What would happen if the human being should still have feelings of fear and anxiety at the onset of Jupiter-consciousness? The outer world at that stage will be far, far more antagonistic and terrible for the human being than is so today. Anyone who does not rid himself here of the habit of anxiety will there fall into one dreadful terror after another.

This condition is already now preparing itself in the outer world. That will show itself still clearer to the human being during the terrible epoch which will come upon us during Oriphiel's rulership, which I spoke to you about last time. When that time comes the human being will need to have learnt to stand firm! Our contemporary culture is itself creating those horrifying monsters which will threaten the human being on Jupiter. You need only look at the huge machines which human technology is today constructing so ingeniously. The human being is creating demons for himself which in the future will rage against him. Everything that he builds today in the way of technical appliances and machines will assume life in the future and oppose him in terrible enmity. Everything that is created for mere utility, to satisfy individual or collective egoism, will be the human being's enemy in the future. We are today far too concerned with gaining useful advantage from what we do. If we really wish to help advance evolution, we should not be concerned with the usefulness of something but with whether it is beautiful and noble. Our actions should not be guided only by utility but by our pure delight in what is beautiful. Everything created by the human being to satisfy his artistic needs, in pure love of beauty, will also assume life in the future and contribute to his higher evolution. It is terrible to see today how many thousands of human beings are forced, from earliest childhood on, to engage only in activities founded upon material utility; they are cut off all their lives from everything that is beautiful and artistic. In the poorest primary school there should hang the finest works of art; that would be an endless blessing for human evolution. The human being is today building his future. One can gain an idea of how things will be on Jupiter if one is clear that today there is no absolute good or absolute evil. In every human being is mixed both good and bad. Whoever is good must recognize that he only has a little more good than bad in himself and is certainly not wholly good. But on Jupiter, good and bad will no longer be combined. Human beings will divide into those who are wholly good and those who are wholly bad. Everything beautiful and noble that we cultivate today leads to a strengthening of the good on Jupiter; everything that occurs as a result of egoism and utility leads to a strengthening of the bad.

In order for the human being to become equal to facing the evil powers of the future, he must take hold of the inmost strength of his 'I'. He must be consciously able to regulate the blood in such a way that it makes him strong in the face of evil, but wholly without anxiety. He must have in his power the strength that directs the blood inwards. But he must also not lose that other capacity of letting the blood stream to the periphery. The Jupiter conditions will represent in a certain sense also a return to the old Moon-consciousness. The human being will regain harmony with the great laws of the universe and feel himself one with them. He will regain the capacity to flow together with the spiritual powers of the universe, yet not in an unconscious and dim way as he did on the Moon. On Jupiter he will always preserve his bright day-consciousness and his self-aware sense of 'I', yet he will live in harmony with the powers and laws of the universe. Discord will resolve itself into harmony. And in order to be able to flow into this universal harmony, he will have to allow consciously the inmost power of his 'I' to shine out from his heart. In other words he must be able consciously to lead the inner forces of the blood towards his centre when confronted by an enemy, and also be able, consciously, to let them shine out. Only then will he be equal to future conditions.

Whoever is striving towards inner development must already today gradually begin to gain control over these forces. This can be done by learning to inhale and exhale consciously. When the human being breathes in, the forces of the 'I' are activated that connect him with the forces of the cosmos, those which shine out from the heart. And when he breathes out, when he deprives himself of breath, the forces of the 'I' are activated that press towards the heart and there make it a firm centre. Thus the pupil can—even today— learn gradually to become master of the forces of his 'I', when he practises conscious breathing as I have indicated. But no one must believe that he should undertake such exercises unaided, if he has not yet received instruction. Each one will be instructed when the time is right for them. But it is never too early, even for those who do not yet practise such exercises, to develop an understanding for their purpose. This will make the exercises all the more productive later on. You should develop more and more understanding, my sisters and brothers, for the subtle processes at work in you and in the universe, and gradually grow into the future ages of human evolution.

(The following given on the same theme, was noted down from the esoteric lesson in Berlin on 26 January 1908)

... When we breathe in deeply and hold our breath, we recapitulate a part of old Moon conditions. When, on the other hand, we leave the breath outside of us, we experience something of Jupiter. The esoteric pupil receives exercises in which he must hold his breath if, in some way, he needs to experience Moon conditions. He receives exercises in which he must leave the breath outside himself if he needs to reach the Jupiter condition. Each person needs to be considered individually.

We know that the river of humanity is already beginning to divide into two streams: one which is drawn towards goodness and morality, and another which will end in dreadfulness and evil. Such conditions are already approaching; their seeds are already present. Everything that exists and is being developed in the world today in the way of machines and appliances will, on Jupiter, become frightful, terrible demons. Everything that serves only to advance the principle of utility will one day come into its own as such awful powers. This process can be paralysed if we transform instruments of utility into those which, besides their usefulness, above all also communicate beauty and godliness. It is very good for us to know this. Otherwise such powers would one day tear the earth asunder. We can also see how enormously important it is in education to surround the child with artistic creations and impressions. Art frees one. Even the locomotive must one day be transformed into a beautiful machine. Our feelings of fear and anxiety nourish other evil beings. We must not allow ourselves to fall prey to such thoughts. On Jupiter such beings will surround us in far greater numbers than they do now. But there is no need for anyone to be alarmed who maintains a clear aura, so that no flies can swarm around the dirt.

V
THE GOSPEL OF KNOWLEDGE
AND ITS PRAYER

Prefatory Note by Marie Steiner

In the four Mystery Plays, Rudolf Steiner gave his knowledge a dramatic form. Spiritual knowledge took form, being enacted by human beings on the stage. The inward striving of the soul towards the spirit was now to be expressed through the actions of personalities. For the ancient Greeks it was a matter of course to weave the figures of the gods into their portrayals of historical events, for the gods were still near to them, experienced by them as living beings. Art was not possible without this realization of the Divine. In our time, however, the law of karma came before the eyes of spirit as a problem of knowledge; it had now to be experienced through deepest feeling. Art is the best way of enabling fellow human beings to share such deep experience. It was a demand of the age that the karma living itself out in the destiny of humanity should be presented in this form. Rudolf Steiner met this demand. After the German spirit had, in the high summer of its classical period, fulfilled its folk-mission, had poured itself out and merged into the world around, the time had now come for the spirit to be individualized, and to anticipate future periods of culture when cultural activities which were becoming fragmented would be brought together once more. It was necessary that the forces of life working in the soul should now lay hold of matter and so penetrate it that it too will become inwardly transparent. Man—in Earth-evolution the last member of the Hierarchies—must now raise himself to them consciously. Until he succeeds he will often fall back into darkness; yet he must not weaken in this striving for the ascent. The paths to this goal are shown to us by art, science and religion, rightly understood.

This knowledge formed the content of the great lectures

given by Dr Steiner immediately after the performances of the Mystery Plays in Munich. The scantiness of the available premises and the desire to provide a building worthy of the Mystery Plays led the listeners to turn their long-cherished wish into a resolve. It was decided to erect the building in Munich, with the co-operation of the artists who found inspiration in these ideas. But the civic authorities, after lengthy negotiations, finally rejected the request.

Our friends now gathered together in free Switzerland and obtained permission for the building to be erected on the Dornach hill in quiet country surroundings, where a few people from Basle had summer homes. This proposal was thankfully accepted. Fate had decided it. The preparatory work began; sketches and the plan of the foundations were drawn and the spot fixed for the cavity in which the Foundation Stone, executed by our friend Max Benzinger, was to be laid. The building that was to rise over it would ensure an open vista of the heavens in all directions.

The Powers working in opposition to advancing human evolution well knew that here a powerful bastion would be erected against their aims. And it was as if they called to their aid the very forces of nature in order to hinder the laying of the Foundation Stone. The elements raged, the rain came down in torrents, the winds stormed. But it would have occurred to no single one of us to think that the day for the laying of the Foundation Stone could be postponed: it was a predestined day.

Filled with the power of the spirit, Dr Steiner's voice rose above the raging elements and penetrated into the hearts of the friends who stood there closely clustered around him — one of whom succeeded in taking down his words in writing, even if with gaps. And so the memory of this day, 20 September 1913, can be preserved for times to come.

The Laying of the Foundation Stone of the First Goetheanum at Dornach, 20 September 1913

My dear sisters and brothers,
Let us today, on this festival evening, understand one another truly. Let us understand that this action really imports for our souls a vow. Our endeavours have brought it about that here, at this place, whence we look far out in the four elemental directions of the heavenly rose, we are permitted to erect this emblem of spiritual life for the new age. Let us understand that on this day, feeling our souls united with that which we have laid symbolically into the earth, we faithfully dedicate ourselves to this spiritual stream in the evolution of mankind which we have recognized as right. Let us try, my dear sisters and brothers, to make this vow in our souls: that in this moment we will look away from all the minutiae of life, from all that binds us — must of necessity bind us — as human beings to the daily round. Let us try in this moment to awaken in ourselves the thought of all that links the human soul with the great struggle at the turning-point of time. Let us try to think for a moment that, as we do what we have vowed to do this evening, we must bear within us the consciousness of looking into far, far cycles of time, in order to become aware of how the mission, of which this building is to be the emblem, will take its place in the great mission of humanity upon our planet earth. Not in pride and vainglory ... in humility, devotion and readiness for sacrifice, let us try to lift our souls to the great plans, the great purposes of man's activity on earth. Let us try to put ourselves into the attitude that we really ought to adopt and must adopt if we understand this moment aright.

Let us try to think how there once entered into our Earth-evolution the great announcement, the great communication, the primeval, eternal gospel of divine spiritual life, how it passed over the earth at a time when the divine Spirits themselves were still the great Teachers of mankind. Let us try, my dear sisters and brothers, to transfer ourselves back into those sacred ages of earth-existence, of which a last yearning, a very last memory, still ascends to us when, maybe in ancient Greece, together with the last echoes of the Mystery-wisdom and simultaneously with the first tones of philosophy, we listen to the great Plato telling of the eternal ideas and the eternal sheaths of the world. And let us try to grasp what since those times has spread over our Earth-evolution as luciferic and ahrimanic influences. Let us try to make clear to ourselves how the connection with the Divine Cosmic Existence, with the willing, with the feeling and with the divine-spiritual knowing, has faded from the human soul.

Let us try in this moment to feel deep, deep in our own souls what in the countries of the East, the West, the South, those human souls whom we acknowledge as the noblest are feeling today, though they get no farther than, let us say, a vague, inadequate longing and hoping for the spirit. Look around you, my dear sisters and brothers, and see how this undefined longing, this vague hoping for the spirit, prevails throughout mankind today. Feel, and hearken, hear by the Foundation Stone of the emblem of our vow how in the vague yearning and hoping of mankind for the spirit there is audible the cry for the answer, for that answer which can be given where spiritual science can be present, with its gospel of the knowledge of the spirit. Try to engrave into your souls the greatness of the moment through which we are passing this evening. If we can hear the longing call of mankind for the spirit and resolve to erect the true building from out of which the tidings of the spirit shall ever more and more be proclaimed—if we feel this in the life of this our world, then we understand one another truly this evening. Then we know — not in pride and in no wise over-valuing our own efforts, but in humility, in devotion and readiness for sacrifice — that in our indefatigable endeavours we must be the continuers of that spiritual work which has been extinguished in the West in the course of advancing human evolution. Inevitably, through the adverse influence of the ahrimanic forces, that evolution ended by bringing mankind to the point where it stands today, the point where souls could only wither and waste away should that cry of longing for the spirit go unheard. My dear sisters and brothers, let us feel this anxiety! It must be so if — aglow with the fire of love — we are to fight on in that great spiritual conflict it is granted us to inherit, in that great spiritual conflict which was waged by our forefathers when they were repelling over there the ahrimanic onslaught of the Moors.

Led by karma, we stand at this moment at a place through which important streams of spiritual life have flowed; let us feel within ourselves this evening the full gravity of the situation. Humanity had in days gone by reached the culminating point in its striving for personality. When in the fullness of this earthly personality the ancient heritage, received from the Divine Leaders of the very beginning of Earth-evolution, had exhausted itself, over there in the East the Cosmic Word appeared:

> In the Beginning was the Word
> And the Word was with God
> And a God was the word.

And the Word was made manifest to the souls of men and spoke to the souls of men: Fill Earth-evolution with the purpose and meaning of the earth! Now the Word Itself has passed over into the earth-aura, has been received into the spiritual aura of the earth.

Fourfold has been the proclamation of the Cosmic Word through the centuries numbering now well-nigh two thousand years. Thus has the Light of Cosmic Worlds shone into Earth-evolution.

Deeper and ever deeper Ahriman sank, and had perforce to sink. Let us feel ourselves surrounded by the souls of men in whom the cry of yearning for the spirit resounds. But let us feel, my dear sisters and brothers, how these human souls all round us might be left crying out in vain, since Ahriman, dark Ahriman, is spreading chaos over all spiritual knowledge of the worlds of the higher Hierarchies for which they strive. Feel that in our time the possibility has indeed arisen of adding to the Spirit-Word, four times proclaimed, that other proclamation which I can now present — but in symbol only.

From the East it came — the Light and the Word of the Proclamation. From out of the East it passed over to the West, four times proclaimed in the four Gospels, awaiting the advent from the West of the mirror that will add knowledge to what is still only proclamation in the four-times uttered Cosmic Word. It pierces deeply into our hearts and souls when we listen to that Sermon on the Mount, which was uttered in the hour when the time for the ripening of human personality was fulfilled, when the ancient Light of the Spirit had vanished and the new Spirit-Light appeared. The new Spirit-Light has appeared! But after it appeared, it travelled through the centuries of human evolution from East to West, waiting for understanding of the words that once in the Sermon on the Mount had sounded their way into human hearts. Deep-toned rings out of the depths of our cosmic evolution that immemorial, undying prayer, uttered as proclamation of the Cosmic Word when the Mystery of Golgotha was enacted. Deep-toned rang out the undying prayer which from the innermost core of the human heart was to make known to the microcosm, in depths of soul, the secret of existence. That secret was to be heard in the Lord's Prayer, as we know it, and as it reverberated from East towards

West. Yet it waited patiently, this Cosmic Word which sank then into the microcosm — waited in order that one day it might resound in harmony with the Fifth Gospel; for the souls of men had to ripen before they could understand that which, as the most ancient of all, because it is the Macrocosmic Gospel, is now to reverberate from the West like an echo to the Gospel of the East.

If we bring understanding to this present moment, then understanding will also dawn in us that to the Four Gospels a Fifth Gospel can be added. So, on this present evening, may there ring forth to the secrets of the microcosm; the words which express the secrets of the macrocosm. As a first revelation of the Fifth Gospel there shall even now sound forth the primeval Macrocosmic World Prayer which is connected with the Moon and Jupiter, even as the Four Gospels are connected with the earth:

AUM, Amen!
Evils prevail,
Evincing the Ego's struggling free,
Debt for selfhood at
    others' expense,
Enjoyed in the daily bread,
Wherein the heavens' will
    prevaileth not,
Since mankind severed
    themselves from Your Kingdom,
And forgot Your Names,
Ye Fathers in the Heavens.

AUM, Amen!
Es walten die Übel,
Zeugen sich lösender Ichheit,
Von andern erschuldete
    Selbstheitschuld,
Erlebet im täglichen Brote,
In dem nicht waltet
    der Himmel Wille,

Da der Mensch sich schied
  von Eurem Reich
Und vergass Euren Namen,
Ihr Väter in den Himmeln.

The 'Our Father' had been given as Prayer to Mankind. There now resounds in answer to the Microcosmic Paternoster, which was proclaimed from the East to the West, the primeval Macrocosmic Prayer. So does it echoing sound, when, rightly understood by human souls, the prayer rings out into cosmic spaces and is given back with the Words imprinted from out of the Macrocosm. Let us take it with us, the Macrocosmic Lord's Prayer, feeling that with it we begin to acquire understanding for the Gospel of Knowledge: the Fifth Gospel. From this weighted moment let us take home earnestly and worthily in our souls—our *will.* Let us take home the certainty that all wisdom for which the human soul is seeking—if the seeking be true—is a reflex of cosmic wisdom, and that it makes fruitful from out of the Love that is sovereign in the evolution of mankind all of human love that is rooted in the soul's own selfless love.

Throughout all earthly ages and into all men's souls there works out of strong human will that has filled itself with the meaning of existence and the meaning of the earth a further strengthening—a strengthening through the Cosmic Power for which men crave today, casting uncertain glances towards a spirit for which they hope—but which they refuse to know, because Ahriman has buried an unconscious fear in the human soul, wherever the spirit is spoken of today. Let us feel this, my sisters and brothers, at this moment. Feel this, and you will be able to arm yourselves for your spiritual task, and as revealers of the Spirit-Light 'will prove yourselves strong in thought, even in the hour when dark Ahriman, clouding wisdom, means to spread the darkness of chaos over fully awakened spiritual sight'.

My sisters and brothers, fill your souls with the longing

for real knowledge of the spirit, for true human love, for strength of will. And try to quicken in yourselves that spirit which has trust in the utterance of the Cosmic Word as it echoes to us out of cosmic distances and out of the wide expanse of space, sounding into our souls. This is what one who has grasped the meaning of existence must truly feel in this evening hour: human souls have reached the limit of their striving. Feel in humility, not in pride, in devotion and willingness for sacrifice, not in arrogant presumption, what is to come of the emblem for which we have laid the Foundation Stone today. Feel this portent of the knowledge which should come to us because it is given to us to know: in our time, the veil enshrouding the spiritual Beings in the expanses of space must be pierced through, as the spiritual Beings come to speak to us of the meaning of existence. Everywhere, everywhere in the surrounding world the souls of men must needs receive into themselves the meaning of existence. Hear how, in whatever cultural centres there is talk of or knowledge of the spirit, of religion, of art, as these things are now understood, the energies of souls are growing more and more barren. Feel how you must learn to quicken these souls, these energies, out of imaginations, inspirations, intuitions of the spirit. Feel what he will find who hears aright the ring of creative spirituality.

Those who in addition to the old Lord's Prayer learn to understand the meaning of the Prayer from the Fifth Gospel, they will recognize the root of that meaning in the crisis of our time.

If we learn to understand the meaning of these words, we shall seek to receive into ourselves the seeds that must blossom now if Earth-evolution is not to wither, if it is still to bear fruit and thrive, so that through the will of man the earth can reach the goal set her from the very Beginning.

Feel, then, this evening, that the wisdom and the meaning of the new knowledge, of the new love and of the great new strength must come alive in the souls of men. The souls who will be working amid the blossoming and the fruits of future ages of Earth-evolution will have to understand that which we today mean to implant in our souls for the first time: the Macrocosmic, re-echoing voice of the ageless, eternal Prayer:

AUM Amen!
Evils prevail,
Evincing the Ego's struggling free,
Debt for selfhood at others' expense,
Enjoyed in the daily bread,
Wherein the heavens' will prevaileth not,
Since mankind severed themselves from Your Kingdom
And forgot Your Names,
Ye Fathers in the Heavens.

Thus we will go our separate ways — taking with us in our souls the consciousness of the meaning, of the earnestness and of the dignity of the solemn act we have performed — the consciousness which should remain of this evening ... kindling in ourselves the striving for knowledge of a New Revelation given to humanity, for which the human soul thirsts, from which it will drink. But only then when, without fear, it wins faith and confidence in what the science of the spirit can make known, the science that is to unite once more those three that, for a time, perforce took their several roads through the evolution of mankind: religion, art and science. Let us take this with us my sisters and brothers, as a token of this hour we have celebrated together, and as something we would wish never to forget.

(Then the Foundation Stone was covered over and cemented in.)

VI
EXEGESIS TO *LIGHT ON THE PATH*
by Mabel Collins

I

The following explanations by Rudolf Steiner refer to the opening sentences of *Light on the Path*:

> These rules were written for all disciples; attend thou to them!
> Before the eyes can see they must be incapable of tears.
> Before the ear can hear it must have lost its sensitiveness.
> Before the voice can speak in the presence of the Masters, it must have lost the power to wound. Before the soul can stand in the presence of the Masters, its feet must be washed in the blood of the heart.

What is called 'truth' by the intellectual soul (Kama Manas) directed towards the finite is only a subspecies of what the esotericist *seeks* as 'the Truth'. For the intellect's truth applies to what *has become*, to what is *manifest*. And the manifested is only a part of Being. Every object in our surroundings is at once product (i.e. become, manifested) and *seed* (unmanifested, becoming). And only when one thinks of an object as both 'become' and 'becoming' does one realize that it is a member of the *one life*, the life where time is not outside, but within it. Thus finite truth is only something that has *become*; it must be called to life by a truth that is becoming. The former one grasps, the latter one 'heeds'. All merely scientific truth belongs to the former kind. *Light on the Path* has not been written for those who seek only this kind of truth. It is written for those who seek the truth which today is seed, in order tomorrow to be product, and who do not grasp the 'become' but heed the 'becoming'. Anyone who wishes to understand the teachings of *Light on the Path* must engender them as his own, and yet love them as something completely independent, as a

---

*See note on page 141.

mother engenders her child as her own and loves it as someone apart.

When the first four precepts are understood, they open the door that leads to esotericism.

What does a man bring to the objects he seeks to know? If he examines himself he will find that pleasure and pain are *his* answer to the impressions of the sense-world and the supersensible world. It is so easy for anyone to believe that he has laid aside inclination and disinclination. But he must descend into the most hidden corners of his soul and drag up *his likes and dislikes*, for only when all such likes and dislikes are consumed by the bliss of the higher Self is knowledge possible. He may think this would make him a cold, prosaic person. That is not so. A piece of gold remains the same piece of gold — in weight and colour — even though it is fashioned into an ornament. So Kama (the astral body) remains what it is — in content and intensity — even when it is spiritually transformed. The Kama-force is not to be extirpated, but incorporated in the content of the *divine fire.* So the tender responsiveness of the eye should not unburden itself in tears, but should enrich the impressions it receives. Dissolve every tear and lend its sparkling brilliance to the ray that penetrates the eye. *Thy* pleasure and *thy* pain are wasted strength, wasted for knowledge. For the force that is expended in this pleasure and pain should stream into the object of knowledge.

Before the eye can see, it must be incapable of tears

Anyone who still abhors the criminal in the customary sense, and still idolizes the saint in that sense, has not rendered his eyes incapable of tears. Consume all thy tears in the will to help. Do not weep over someone stricken with poverty; get to know his situation and help him! Do not grumble about what is bad; understand it and change it into good. Thy tears only dim the pure clarity of the light.

Thy *sensations* are all the more delicate, the less *sensitive* thou art. Sound becomes clear to the ear if its clarity is not disturbed by encountering rapture or sympathetic feeling as it enters the ear.

Before the ear can hear, it must have lost its sensitiveness

Put it another way, this means: let the heartbeats of the other resound in you, and do not disturb them with the beating of your own heart. Open your ear and not your nerve-endings. For these will tell you whether the tone is *agreeable* or not, while your open ear will tell you the tone's true nature. When you go to someone who is ill, let every fibre of *his* body speak to you, and deaden the impression he makes on you.

To take the first two precepts together: reverse your will; let it be as forceful as possible, but do not let it stream into things as *yours*. Rather inform yourself about the things and then impart your will to them; let your will and yourself stream out of the things. Let the light-force of your eyes flow out of every flower, every stone; but hold back yourself and your tears.

Bestow your words on dumb things so that they may speak through you. For they are not a summons to your pleasure, these dumb things, but a summons to your activity. It is not what they have *become* without you that is there for you, but what they are to become through you.

As long as you impress your wish on a single thing without this wish having been born from the thing itself, you are wounding it. But as long as you are wounding anything, no Master can listen to you. For the Master hears only those who need him; and no one who wishes to impress himself upon things has need of the Master. Man's lower self is like a pointed needle that wants to engrave itself everywhere. As long as it wants to do that, no Master will wish to hear its voice.

Before the voice can speak in the presence of the Masters, it must have lost the power to wound.

As long as the sharp needles of the 'I will' project from man's words, so long are his words the emissaries of his lower self. If these needles are removed and the voice becomes soft and pliant, so that it lays itself round the mysteries of all things as a veiling garment, then it weaves itself into Spirit-raimant (Majavirupa), and the Master's delicate tone takes it as vesture. With every thought which in the true sense of the word a man dedicates to the inner truth of things, he weaves a thread of the garment in which the Master who appears to him may wrap himself. One who makes himself an envoy of the world, an organ through whom the depths of the world-riddle speak, 'pours out the life of his soul in the world'; his heart's blood leaves his feet so that they may haste in carrying him to where there is work to be done. And when the soul is where the lower 'I' is *not*, when it is not where man stands enjoying pleasant things, but where his active feet have borne him, then the Master appears there too.

Before the soul can stand in the presence of the Masters, the feet must be washed in the blood of the heart

He who remains in himself cannot find the Master; he who would find him must let the strength of his soul — his heart's blood – flow into all he does, into his active feet.

Here is the *first* meaning of the four fundamental precepts. To someone who lives with this first meaning, the second meaning can be unveiled, and then the succeeding ones. For these occult precepts are occult truths and every occult truth has at least a sevenfold meaning.

II

The second part of the exegesis refers to Chapter II of *Light on the Path*, paragraph 17:

Inquire of the inmost, the One, its final secret which it holds for you through the ages.

The great and difficult struggle, the conquering of the desires of the individual soul, is a work of ages; therefore do not expect to gain the prize of victory until ages of experience have been accumulated. When the time of actually mastering this seventeenth lesson is reached, man is on the threshold of becoming more than man.

Wisdom of the deepest kind is embodied in these last paragraphs of the second chapter of *Light on the Path*. Paragraph 17 includes the challenge, 'Inquire of the inmost, the One, its final secret'. He who illumines the depths of his 'inmost' finds indeed the results of 'ages'. For what man is today, that has he become through thousands of years. This inmost has passed through worlds, and in its womb lie hidden the fruits it has brought with it from these worlds. Our inmost being owes what it now is to the fact that countless formative influences have worked at its structure; that it has passed through many kingdoms and from these has again and again formed itself into organs. Through these organs it could interact with the worlds that formed its environment from time to time. And what it has gained from this intercourse it has taken over into new worlds, in order that thus equipped from the past it might pass on to further stages of ever richer experiences. And so today we make use of the essential kernel of our inmost being in its differentiations in order to have a summation of experiences on the 'planet' we call 'Earth'.

All that we passed through on the 'Moon-planet' and earlier planets is in our inmost being. These experiences were already in this inmost part as it evolved onwards through a Pralaya to the stage of 'Earth'. They were in the

Pitri-nature[1] of this inmost part as the whole lily is latent in the seed, though the seed, of course, is physically visible. The 'Pitri-seed' that slept over from 'Moon' to 'Earth' was incarnated in substances of the highest order, perceptible only to the 'Dangma's[2] Opened Eye'. When the lily seed is sown in the ground, it so orders the substance of earth, water and air that a new lily is formed. Similarly, the Pitri-seed in its cycles through Earth existence so orders substance that in the course of those cycles the perfected human being gradually arises, until after the Sixth Earth Round and by the beginning of the Seventh he may truly be called the 'Likeness of God'. Up to the middle of the Fourth Round—up to the end of the Lemurian Age—the human Pitri-nature shared in the work on its own organism with 'sculptors' of a more and less exalted kind; but from this point of time onward man's inmost being has to take over this work itself. K.H.[3] says the following about this work: All that 'thou' has to do is to become 'complete Man'. For know: only in thy physical nature art thou already—nearly—Man. For only at the end of the Fourth Round wilt thou become fully Man even in thy physical nature. Still unorganized, still chaotic, however, are thy astral body, thy mental body and thy ego-body (higher Manas). Just as perfected as thy physical body after the Fourth must thy astral body be after the Fifth, thy mental body after the Sixth and thy arupa body (higher mental body) after the Seventh Round, when at the end of earthly cycles thou shouldst have attained thy destiny. And only when thou hast

---

1 Lunar-Pitri is the Eastern term for the Beings referred to as 'Angels' in the book *Occult Science: An Outline*, and belonging to the Hierarchy immediately above man. They passed through their human stage on the Old Moon and are now at the stage man will have reached when the Earth's evolution is completed.

2 Dangma = seer.

3 'K.H.' = Koot Hoomi, one of the Eastern Masters spoken of in the Theosophical Society.

attained *this* destiny canst thou, as normal terrestrial Pitri, move on to the next planet.

Those, however, who wish to take the occult path should consciously and continuously work from their inmost being upon the organizing of these three higher bodies. That is the point of meditating.

The *astral body* is organized through raising oneself to the higher Self and through self-examination. In long past Rounds, forces outside man were at work, building the physical body's organs as they are today. In the same way the higher Self within man is working on the astral body so that it may become a 'likeness of the Godhead' or 'complete man'. The astral body then becomes capable of experiencing the mysteries of higher worlds through *its* organs, as the physical body experiences the secrets of the physical-mineral world through its own sense-organs. We examine ourselves at night as to our day's experiences. We raise ourselves to our 'higher Self' through the familiar formula. In both activities we are working on our astral body in an organizing, constructive way. Only thus do we make it into an astral organism, a body with organs, whereas before it was only a kind of bearer. The formula is this:

More radiant than the sun,	*Strahlender als die Sonne,*
Purer than the snow,	*Reiner als der Schnee,*
Finer than the ether	*Feiner als der Äther,*
Is the Self,	*Ist das Selbst,*
The spirit in my	*Der Geist inmitten*
heart of hearts.	*meines Herzens.*
I am this Self.	*Ich bin dieses Selbst.*
This Self am I.	*Dieses Selbst bin Ich.*

A vista is indeed opened through it on to 'a work of ages', as is further said in paragraph 17. Just as thousands of years were needed to attain the external physical stage of 'likeness', so will a work of millennia be required before this likeness can be attained for the higher bodies.

Only then does man stand on the 'threshold of becoming more than man'. And he must come to this threshold in the Seventh Round, as at the end of the lunar period (Moon) he had to be at the threshold which raised him beyond the stage of Lunar-Pitri.

Through mental meditation on a sentence from the inspired scripts, the person who meditates organizes his mental body. To take such sentences from the *Bhagavadgita*, or from other writings found in theosophical literature, is to work on the organizing of this mental body. It must be repeatedly emphasized that it is far less a matter of going through the sentence intellectually — that should be done for its own sake apart from the actual meditation — than of *living* with the sentence in a completely free field of consciousness. The sentence itself should say to us what it has to say to us. We should be the receivers. If it is an inspired sentence, then it begins to live in our consciousness; its living element streams forth, it becomes in us a fullness, a content undreamt of before. As long as we speculate about it, we can put into it only what is in us already. And in that way we get no further.

The organization of the ego-body depends on the devotional extent of our meditation. The greater our attainment through this devotion, and the deeper, more earnest it is, the more do we become like the Being who will be ourself as we move out of the life of our planet to the tasks which lie before us in a later existence.

III

The explanations now to be given refer to paragraph 18:

> The knowledge which is now yours is yours only because your soul has become one with all pure souls and with the inmost. It is a trust vested in you by the Most High. Betray it, misuse your knowledge, let it drowse when you should be exerting it, and it is possible even now for you to fall from the high estate you

have attained. Great ones fall back, even from the threshold, unable to sustain the weight of their responsibility, unable to pass on. Therefore look forward always with awe and trembling to this moment and be prepared for the battle.

We must come to realize that we are one with all that lives. We must be clear that what we call our private individuality has no life if it tries to keep apart from others. Then it has no more life than our little finger would have if it were cut off from the whole organism. And what the physical-material severing would be for our little finger, that, for our individuality, would be a knowledge that wished to concern itself only with this individuality. We were *one* when, within an all-divine Being, we entered upon the planet that was the first of three to precede our earth; we were within the all-divine Being and yet individual, as each tone in a symphony is individual and yet one with the whole symphony. What we are summoned to call our individuality must let itself be worked upon by what it encounters in the 343 worlds which it lives through (seven planets, seven rounds on each planet, seven so-called Globes to each Round = 7 × 7 × 7 metamorphoses = 343).

What we are thus enabled to experience is laid in us as *foundation* from the *very first*. And that is the treasure 'entrusted to thee by the Most High'. And as the treasure is entrusted to us, so are we to place it in the harmony of the planetary symphony. Anyone who fully understands *these* things will again and again meet with a certain experience. All deepening in our inner being remains unfruitful, empty, if we desire it only for ourselves. To strive for *our* personal perfection is really only pandering to a higher egotism. Our knowledge must continually flow from us. This does not mean that we must positively teach all the time. That is something for each person to do as he can and when he can. But in everyday life the living result of selflessly acquired knowledge can be felt in the lightest hand-clasp.

When we do really perceive that all life is one, that all isolation is based on Maya, then all our inward deepening will be imbued with the lively feeling that we are to carry it actively into the All-one life. And then our deepening is always rewarded by fruitfulness. We are then sure that we cannot fall back. Anyone who is striving for knowledge solely for the sake of his own perfection, solely that he may advance on the ladder of existence, can still fall, even when he has already mounted very high. Above all we must be conscious of the 'responsibility' that we take upon ourselves through gaining higher knowledge. Only a certain measure of potential development is allotted to mankind as a whole on the path of evolution. If therefore we make ourselves more perfect, if we appropriate to ourselves a measure of perfection earlier than would be possible in normal progress, we are *taking* for ourselves something from the common measure of mankind. We make the scales dip on our side; up flies the balance on the other side. Only through giving in one way or another can we make good what we have *taken*. We must not think, however, that it would be better not to take. That again means egotism, abstaining from taking in order to be spared the burden of giving.

Not to take and not to give signifies *death*. But we are to *serve life*. We must acquire the faculty of giving and must therefore burden ourselves with the responsibility of taking. We must be aware of this responsibility at every moment; when we have taken we must constantly consider how we can best give.

This produces a 'battle', an earnest, solemn battle. Yet this battle must be; we *may not* shun it and must arm ourselves for it continually. The lofty significance of this battle has always been and always will be brought especially before the mystics of all Schools of Initiation. They were exhorted to fill themselves, permeate themselves, with consciousness of this conflict. If the conflict becomes the very breath of our being, a fundamental mood of soul, then inner sight and inner hearing are freshly animated. And if we are able to be calm, *quite calm* on this battleground, then the lightning of higher mysteries begins to flash in our astral and mental sky. Feelings, thoughts, clothe themselves in symbols that are spiritually palpable realities, and from out of the nimbus of these spiritually palpable realities the voice of the Master sounds, his form is fashioned. The higher *intercourse* has begun for us. We begin to be no longer merely co-actors in the world but are messengers for it (Angelos).

This exegesis of paragraph 18 is sentence for sentence reality, higher reality to be experienced. And one who permeates himself with the meaning of this paragraph in this way becomes a citizen of higher worlds.

NOTE

Light on the Path, by the English theosophist Mabel Collins (1851–1927), was first published by the Theosophical Society in the 1880s and translated into German by Baron Oskar von Hoffman during the same decade. It is described on its title page as 'A treatise written for the personal use of those who are ignorant of the Eastern wisdom and who desire to enter within its influence, written down by M.C.', with notes and comments by the author'. It consists of two chapters of 'Rules for all Disciples', followed by notes keyed to certain sentences in the Rules and four chapters of comments, with a final chapter on Karma. The words, 'written down by M.C.', indicate that the Rules and Notes were received inspirationally. The comments, by the author herself, first appeared in H.P. Blavatsky's journal, *Lucifer*, volume I, 1887–88.

Rudolf Steiner wrote the first part of his exegesis at Christmas 1903 and the second part in the following summer. Appended to the second part is a note, 'To be continued as soon as possible', but the occasion for this further exegesis never came.

VII
MODERN AND ANCIENT
SPIRITUAL EXERCISES

ADVICE ON MEDITATION

Modern and Ancient Spiritual Exercises*

Dornach, 27 May 1922

The paths by which in very remote times men acquired supersensible knowledge were very different from those appropriate today. I have often drawn attention to the fact that in ancient times man possessed a faculty of instinctive clairvoyance. This clairvoyance went through many different phases to become what may be described as modern man's consciousness of the world, a consciousness out of which a higher one can be developed. In my books *Occult Science: An Outline* and *Knowledge of the Higher Worlds: How is it Achieved?* and other writings is described how man at present, when he understands his own times, can attain higher knowledge.

When we look back to the spiritual strivings of man in a very distant past we find among others the one practised in the Orient within the culture known later as the Ancient Indian civilization. Many people nowadays are returning to what was practised then because they cannot rouse themselves to the realization that, in order to penetrate into supersensible worlds, every epoch must follow its own appropriate path.

On previous occasions I have mentioned that, from the masses of human beings who lived during the period described in my *Occult Science* as the Ancient Indian epoch, certain individuals developed, in a manner suited to that age, inner forces which led them upwards into supersensible worlds. One of the methods followed is known as

* Abridged from *The Human Soul in Relation to World Evolution*, published by Anthroposophic Press, 1984.

the path of yoga; I have spoken about this path on other occasions.

The path of yoga can best be understood if we first consider the people in general from among whom the yogi emerged — that is to say, the one who sets out to attain higher knowledge by this path. In those remote ages of mankind's evolution, human consciousness in general was very different from what it is today. In the present age we look out into the world and through our senses perceive colours, sounds and so on. We seek for laws of nature prevailing in the physical world and we are conscious that if we attempt to experience a spirit-soul content in the external world then we add something to it in our imagination. It was different in the remote past for then, as we know, man saw more in the external world than ordinary man sees today. In lightning and thunder, in every star, in the beings of the different kingdoms of nature, the men of those times beheld spirit and soul. They perceived spiritual beings even if of a lower kind, in all solid matter, in everything fluid or aeriform. Today's intellectual outlook declares that these men of old, through their fantasy, dreamed all kinds of spiritual and psychical qualities into the world around them. This is known as animism.

We little understand the nature of man, especially that of man in ancient times, if we believe that the spiritual beings manifesting in lightning and thunder, in springs and rivers, in wind and weather, were dream-creations woven into nature by fantasy. This was by no means the case. Just as we perceive red or blue and hear C sharp or G, so those men of old beheld realities of spirit and soul in external objects. For them it was as natural to see spirit-soul entities as it is for us to see colours and so on. However, there was another aspect to this way of experiencing the world, namely, that man in those days had no clear consciousness of self.

The clear self-consciousness which permeates the normal human being today did not yet exist. Though he did not express it, man did not, as it were, distinguish himself from the external world. He felt as my hand would feel were it conscious: that it is not independent, but an integral part of the organism. Men felt themselves to be members of the whole universe. They had no definite consciousness of their own being as separate from the surrounding world. Suppose a man of that time was walking along a river bank. If someone today walks along a river bank downstream he, as modern, clever man, feels his legs stepping out in that direction and this has nothing whatever to do with the river. In general, the man of old did not feel like that. When he walked along a river downstream, as was natural for him to do, he was conscious of the spiritual beings connected with the water of the river flowing in that direction. Just as a swimmer today feels himself carried along by the water — that is, by something material — so the man of old felt himself guided downstream by something spiritual. That is only an example chosen at random. In all his experiences of the external world man felt himself to be supported and impelled by gods of wind, river and all surrounding nature. He felt the elements of nature within himself. Today this feeling of being at one with nature is lost. In its place man has acquired a strong feeling of his independence, of his individual 'I'.

The yogi rose above the level of the masses whose experiences were as described. He carried out certain exercises of which I shall speak. These exercises were good and suitable for the nature of humanity in ancient times; they have later fallen into decadence and have mainly been used for harmful ends. I have often referred to these yoga breathing exercises. Therefore, what I am now describing was a method for the attainment of higher worlds that was suitable and right only for man in a very ancient oriental civilization.

In ordinary life breathing functions unconsciously. We breathe in, hold the breath and exhale; this becomes a conscious process only if in some way we are not in good health. In ordinary life, breathing remains for the most part an unconscious process. But during certain periods of his exercises the yogi transformed his breathing into a conscious inner experience. This he did by timing the inhaling, holding and exhaling of the breath differently and so altered the whole rhythm of the normal breathing. In this way the breathing process became conscious. The yogi projected himself, as it were, into his breathing. He felt himself one with the indrawn breath, with the spreading of the breath through the body and with the exhaled breath. In this way he was drawn with his whole soul into the breath.

In order to understand what is achieved by this let us look at what happens when we breathe. When we inhale, the breath is driven into the organism, up through the spinal cord, into the brain; from there it spreads out into the system of nerves and senses. Therefore, when we think, we by no means depend only on our senses and nervous system as instruments of thinking. The breathing process pulsates and beats through them with its perpetual rhythm. We never think without this whole process taking place, of which we are normally unaware because the breathing remains unconscious.

The yogi, by altering the rhythm of the breath, drew it consciously into the process of nerves and senses. Because the altered breathing caused the air to billow and whirl through the brain and nerve-sense system, the result was an inner experience of their function when combined with the air. As a consequence, he also experienced a soul element in his thinking within the rhythm of breathing.

Something extraordinary happened to the yogi by this means. The process of thinking, which he had hardly felt as a function of the head at all, streamed into his whole organism. He did not merely think, but felt the thought as a little live creature that ran through the whole process of breathing which he had artificially induced.

Thus, the yogi did not feel thinking to be merely a shadowy, logical process; he rather felt how thinking followed the breath. When he inhaled he felt he was taking something from the external world into himself which he then let flow with the breath into his thinking. With his thoughts he took hold, as it were, of that which he had inhaled with the air and spread through his whole organism. The result of this was that there arose in the yogi an enhanced feeling of his own 'I', an intensified feeling of self. He felt his thinking pervading his whole being. This made him aware of his thinking particularly in the rhythmic air-current within him.

This had a very definite effect upon the yogi. When man today is aware of himself within the physical world he quite rightly does not pay attention to his thinking as such. His senses inform him about the external world and when he looks back upon himself he perceives at least a portion of his own being. This gives him a picture of how man is placed within the world between birth and death. The yogi radiated the ensouled thoughts into the breath. This soul-filled thinking pulsated through his inner being with the result that there arose in him an enhanced feeling of self-hood. But in this experience he did not feel himself living between birth and death in the physical world surrounded by nature. He felt carried back in memory to the time before he descended to the earth, that is, to the time when he was a spiritual-soul being in a spiritual-soul world.

In normal consciousness today man can reawaken experiences of the past. He may, for instance, have a vivid recollection of some event that took place ten years ago in a wood perhaps; he distinctly remembers all the details, the whole mood and setting. In just the same way did the yogi, through his changed breathing, feel himself drawn back into the wood and atmosphere, into the whole setting of a spiritual-soul world in which he had been as a spiritual-soul being. There he felt quite differently about the world than he felt in his normal consciousness. The result of the changed relationship of the now awakened selfhood to the whole universe gave rise to the wonderful poems of which the *Bhagavadgita* is a beautiful example.

In the *Bhagavadgita* we read wonderful descriptions of how the human soul, immersed in the phenomena of nature, partakes of every secret, steeping itself in the mysteries of the world. These descriptions are all reproductions of memories, called up by means of yoga breathing, of the soul—when it was as yet only soul—and lived within a spiritual universe. In order to read the ancient writings such as the *Bhagavadgita* with understanding one must be conscious of what speaks through them. The soul, with enhanced feeling of selfhood, is transported into its past in the spiritual world and is relating what Krishna and other ancient initiates had experienced there through their heightened self-consciousness.

Thus, it can be said that those sages of old rose to a higher level of consciousness than that of the masses of people. The initiates strictly isolated the 'self' from the external world. This came about, not for any egotistical reason, but as a result of the changed process of breathing in which the soul, as it were, dived down into the rhythm of the inner air current. By this method a path into the spiritual world was sought in ancient times.

Later this path underwent modifications. In very ancient times the yogi felt how in the transformed breathing his thoughts were submerged in the currents of breath, running through them like little snakes. He felt himself to be part of a weaving cosmic life and this feeling expressed itself in certain words and sayings. It was noticeable that one spoke differently when these experiences were revealed through speech. What I have described was gradually felt less intensely within the breath; it no longer remained within the breathing process itself. Rather were the words breathed out, and formed of themselves rhythmic speech. Thus the changed breathing led, through the words carried by the breath, to the creation of mantras; whereas, formerly, the process and experience of breathing was the most essential, now these poetic sayings assumed primary importance. They passed over into tradition, into the historical consciousness of man and subsequently gave birth later to rhythm, metre, and so on, in poetry.

The basic laws of speech, which are to be seen, for instance, in the pentameter and hexameter as used in ancient Greece, point back to what had once long before been an experience of the breathing process – an experience which transported man from the world in which he was living between birth and death into a world of spirit and soul.

This is not the path modern man should seek into the spiritual world. He must rise into higher worlds, not by the detour of the breath, but along the more inward path of thinking itself. The right path for man today is to transform, in meditation and concentration, the otherwise merely logical connection between thoughts into something of a musical nature. Meditation today is to begin always with an experience in thought, an experience of the transition from one thought into another, from one mental picture into another.

While the yogi in ancient India passed from one kind of breathing into another, man today must attempt to project himself into a living experience of, for example, the colour red. Thus he remains within the realm of thought. He must then do the same with blue and experience the rhythm: red–blue, blue–red, red–blue and so on, which is a thought-rhythm. But it is not a rhythm that can be found in a logical thought sequence; it is a thinking that is much more alive.

If one perseveres for a sufficiently long time with exercises of this kind (the yogi, too, was obliged to carry out his exercises for a very long time) and really experience the inner qualitative change, and the swing and rhythm of red–blue, blue–red, light–dark, dark–light—in short, if indications such as those given in my book *Knowledge of the Higher Worlds* are followed—the exact opposite is achieved to that of the yogi in ancient times. He blended thinking with breathing, thus turning the two processes into one. The aim today is to dissolve the last connection between the two, which, in any case, is unconscious. The process by which, in ordinary consciousness, we think and form concepts of our natural environment is not only connected with nerves and senses; a stream of breath is always flowing through this process. While we think, the breath continually pulsates through the nerves and senses.

All modern exercises in meditation aim at entirely separating thinking from breathing. Thinking is not on this account torn out of rhythm, because as thinking becomes separated from the inner rhythm of breath it is gradually linked to an external rhythm. By setting thinking free from the breath we let it stream, as it were, into the rhythm of the external world. The yogi turned back into his own rhythm. Today man must return to the rhythm of the external world. In *Knowledge of the Higher Worlds* you will find that one of the first exercises shows how to contemplate the germination and growth of a plant. This meditation works towards separating thinking from the breath and letting it dive down into the growth forces of the plant itself.

Thinking must pass over into the rhythm pervading the external world. The moment thinking really becomes free of the bodily functions, the moment it has torn itself away from breathing and gradually united with the external rhythm, it dives down not into the physical qualities of things but into the spiritual within individual objects.

We look at a plant: it is green and its blossoms are red.

This our eyes tell us and our intellect confirms the fact. This is the reaction of ordinary consciousness. We develop a different consciousness when we separate thinking from breathing and connect it with what exists outside. This thinking yearns to vibrate with the plant as it grows and unfolds its blossoms. This thinking follows how in a rose, for example, green passes over into red. Thinking vibrates within the spiritual which lies at the foundation of each single object in the external world.

This is how modern meditation differs from the yoga exercises practised in very ancient times. There are naturally many intermediate stages; I chose these two extremes. The yogi sank down, as it were, into his own breathing process; he sank into his own self. This caused him to experience this self as if in memory; he remembered what he had been before he came down to earth. We, on the other hand, pass out of the physical body with our soul and unite ourselves with what lives spiritually in the rhythms of the external world. In this way we behold directly what we were before we descended to the earth. This is the consequence of gradually entering into the external rhythm.

To illustrate the difference I will draw it schematically. Let this be the yogi (first drawing, white lines). He developed a strong feeling of his 'I' (red). This enabled him to remember what he was, within a soul-spiritual environment, before he descended to earth (blue). He went back on the stream of memory.

Let this be the modern man who has attained supersensible knowledge (second drawing, white lines). He develops a process that enables him to go out of his body (blue) and live within the rhythm of the external world and behold directly, as an external object (red), what he was before he descended to earth.

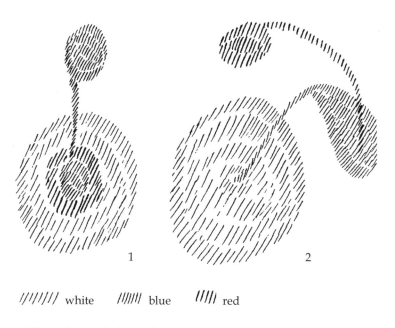

1   2

/////// white   ////// blue   //// red

Thus, knowledge of one's existence before birth was in ancient times in the nature of memory, whereas at the present time a rightly developed cognition of pre-birth existence is a direct beholding of what one was (red). That is the difference.

That was one of the methods by which the yogi attained insight into the spiritual world. Another was by adopting certain positions of the body. One exercise was to hold the arms outstretched for a long time; or he took up a certain position by crossing his legs and sitting on them and so on. What was attained by this?

He attained the possibility to perceive what can be perceived with those senses which today are not even recognized as senses. We know that man has not just five senses but twelve. I have often spoken about this—for example, apart from the usual five he has a sense of balance through which he perceives the equilibrium of his body so that he does not fall to the right or left, or backwards or forwards. Just as we perceive colours, so we must perceive our own balance or we should slip and fall in all directions. Someone who is intoxicated or feels faint loses his balance just because he fails to perceive his equilibrium. In order to make himself conscious of this sense of balance, the yogi adopted certain bodily postures. This developed in him a strong, subtle sense of direction. We speak of above and below, of right and left, of back and front as if they were all the same. The yogi became intensely conscious of their differences by keeping his body for lengthy periods in certain postures. In this way he developed a subtle awareness of the other senses of which I have spoken. When these are experienced they are found to have a much more spiritual character than the five familiar senses. Through them the yogi attained perception of the directions of space.

This faculty must be regained but along a different path. For reasons which I will explain more fully on another occasion the old yoga exercises are unsuitable today. However, we can attain an experience of the qualitative differences within the directions of space by undertaking such exercises in thinking as I have described. They separate thinking from breathing and bring it into the rhythm of the external world. We then experience, for instance, what it signifies that the spine of animals lies in the horizontal direction whereas in man it is vertical. It is well known that the magnetic needle always points north–south. Therefore, on earth the north–south direction means something special, for the manifestation of magnetic forces, since the magnetic needle, which is otherwise neutral, reacts to it. Thus, the north–south direction has a special quality. By penetrating into the external rhythm with our thoughts we learn to recognize what it means when the spine is horizontal or vertical. We remain in the realm of thought and learn through thinking itself. The Indian yogi learned it, too, but by crossing his legs and sitting on them and by keeping his arms raised for a long time. Thus, he learned from the bodily postures the significance of the invisible directions of space. Space is not haphazard, but organized in such a way that the various directions have different values.

The exercises that have been described which lead man into higher worlds are mainly exercises in the realm of thought. There are exercises of an opposite kind; among them are the various methods employed in asceticism. One such method is the suppression of the normal function of the physical body through inflicting pain and all kinds of deprivations. It is practically impossible for modern man to form an adequate idea of the extremes to which such exercises were carried by ascetics in former times. Modern man prefers to be as firmly as possible within his physical body. But whenever the ascetic suppressed some function of the body by means of physical pain, his spirit-soul nature drew out of his organism.

In normal life the soul and spirit of man are connected with the physical organism between birth and death in accordance with the human organization as a whole. When the bodily functions are suppressed, through ascetic practices, something occurs which is similar to when someone today sustains an injury. When one knows how modern man generally reacts to some slight hurt, then it is clear that there is a great difference between that and what the ascetic endured just to make his soul organism free. The ascetic experienced the spiritual world with the soul organism that had been driven out through such practices. Nearly all of the earlier great religious revelations originated in this way.

Those concerned with modern religious life make light of these things. They declare the great religious revelations to be poetic fiction, maintaining that whatever insight man acquires should not cause pain. The seekers of religious truths in former times did not take this view. They were quite clear about the fact that when man is completely bound up with his organism, as of necessity he must be for his earthly tasks — the aim was not to portray unworldliness as an ideal – then he cannot have spiritual experiences. The ascetics in former times sought spiritual experiences by suppressing bodily life and even inflicting pain. Whenever pain drove out spirit and soul from a bodily member, that part which was driven out experienced the spiritual world. The great religions have not been attained without pain but rather through great suffering.

These fruits of human strivings are today accepted through faith. Faith and knowledge are neatly separated. Knowledge of the external world, in the form of natural science, is acquired through the head. As the head has a thick skull, this causes no pain, especially as this knowledge consists of extremely abstract concepts. On the other hand, those concepts handed down as venerable traditions are accepted simply through faith. It must be said though, that basically, knowledge and faith have in common the fact that today one is willing to accept only knowledge that can be acquired painlessly, and faith does not hurt any more than science, though its knowledge was originally attained through great pain and suffering.

Despite all that has been said, the way of the ascetic cannot be the way for present-day man. In our time it is perfectly possible, through inner self-discipline and training of the will, to take in hand one's development which is otherwise left to education and the experiences of life. One's personality can be strengthened by training the will. One can, for example, say to oneself: Within five years I shall acquire a new habit and during that time I shall concentrate my whole will-power upon achieving it. When the will is trained in this way, for the sake of inner perfection, then one loosens, without ascetic practices, the soul-spiritual from the bodily nature. The first discovery, when such training of the will is undertaken for the sake of self-improvement, is that a continuous effort is needed. Every day something must be achieved inwardly. Often it is only a slight accomplishment but it must be pursued with iron determination and unwavering will. It is often the case that if, for example, such an exercise as concentration each morning upon a certain thought is recommended, people will embark upon it with burning enthusiasm. But it does not last, the will slackens and the exercise becomes mechanical because the strong energy which is increasingly required is not forthcoming. The first resistance to be overcome is one's own lethargy; then comes the other resistance, which is of an objective nature, and it is as if one had to fight one's way through a dense thicket. After that, one reaches the experience that hurts because thinking, which has gradually become strong and alive, has found its way into the rhythm of the external world and begins to perceive the direction of space — in fact, perceive what is alive. One discovers that higher knowledge is attainable only through pain.

I can well picture people today who want to embark upon the path leading to higher worlds. They make a start and the first delicate spiritual cognition appears. This causes pain so they say they are ill; when something causes pain one must be ill. However, the attainment of higher knowledge will often be accompanied by great pain, yet one is not ill. No doubt it is more comfortable to seek a cure than continue the path. Attempts must be made to overcome this pain of the soul which becomes ever greater as one advances. While it is easier to have something prescribed than continue the exercises, no higher knowledge is attained that way. Provided the body is robust and fit for dealing with external life, as is normally the case at the present time, this immersion in pain and suffering becomes purely an inner soul path in which the body does not participate. When man allows knowledge to approach him in this way, then the pain he endures signifies that he is attaining those regions of spiritual life out of which the great religions were born. The great religious truths which fill our soul with awe, conveying as they do those lofty regions in which, for example, our immortality is rooted, cannot be reached without painful inner experiences. The great truths do indeed demand an inner courage of soul which enables it to say to itself: If you could experience these things you must be prepared to attain knowledge of them through deprivation and suffering. I am not saying this to discourage anyone, but because it is the truth. It may be discouraging for many, but what good would it do to tell people that they can enter higher worlds in perfect comfort when it is not the case. The attainment of higher worlds demands the overcoming of suffering.

I have tried today, my dear friends, to describe to you how it is possible to advance to man's true being. The human soul and spirit lie deeply hidden within him and must be attained. Even if someone does not set out himself on that conquest he must know about what lies hidden within him. He must know about such things as those described yesterday* and how they run their course. This knowledge is a demand of our age. These things can be discovered only along such paths as those I have indicated again today by describing how they were trodden in former times and how they must be trodden now.

---

* Lecture of 26 May, 1922 in *The Human Soul in Relation to World Evolution* (op. cit.).

Advice on Meditation Given by Rudolf Steiner

(recorded by Martina von Limburger)

Meditation and concentration—these are not some sort of marvel, they are spiritual activities, intensified to the highest degree, which also occur in ordinary life in their elementary stages. Meditation is a surrender of the soul, immeasurably enhanced, such as may perhaps be found in the most beautiful feelings of religious life. Concentration is an attentiveness which we also have to employ in ordinary life, only now endlessly intensified. We call it paying attention, when we do not let our ideas and feelings sweep over things just as they like but when we rouse ourselves to direct our interest to one single object. This attention can be intensified to an unlimited extent, particularly by bringing into the centre of our soul-life certain concepts which are given us through spiritual science. In this way the whole life of the soul can be concentrated for a definite time on these concepts at the centre, shutting out everything else, all cares and worries, all sense-impressions and will-impulses, all feeling and all thinking. We must bear in mind, however, that we are not primarily concerned with the *contents* of these concepts, but with the *energy*, the inner activity that we develop in giving ourselves up to them.

The morning, shortly after our waking, has proved the most suitable time for meditating. After waking up we should strive through our meditation to sink back again as soon as possible into the spiritual world, but now consciously, just as in the evening we prepare to enter it.

On awakening one should spend a few moments in spiritual stillness. In so doing one will kindle the holy fire, the inner warmth that is necessary for the effort of the soul.

Yet in the ensuing meditation one should try to shape the thoughts clearly, sharply and definitely, as in an activity of soul taking place in full consciousness and self-possession. At the same time one's physical and etheric organism must remain undisturbed, for in a correct meditation one reaches the point of experiencing oneself outside the physical and etheric organism in the newly developed content of thought-forces...

How long should one meditate? That cannot be expressed in terms of time. One should continue with each meditation as long as one can draw inner strength from it. One should meditate with one's whole being.

Streams of spiritual life are always flowing through the world. Yet as long as we busy ourselves with ordinary everyday thoughts these streams cannot flow into us. Our meditation-words are like gateways into the spiritual world; they are winged messengers which bear men upwards into supersensible realms. They have power to unlock our soul so that the thoughts of our great leaders, the 'Masters of Wisdom and the Harmony of Feelings', can stream into us. For this to happen, the deepest inner silence must prevail. The words which we let live in our soul after waking and which have been given us by the great teachers of mankind should not be used as matter for speculation. The rest of the day gives us time to think over them. During meditation we should keep at a distance any reflecting on the content of these words. And yet we must not repeat them merely in a meaningless, mechanical way. Rather should we be quite clear that the words open our souls to the instreaming of divine beings, as the chalice of the flower opens to receive the rays of the sun. High spirit-beings stream down to us during our meditation, above all, however, the thoughts of those whom we call the Masters of mankind. They guide us and are near to us when we meditate.

If our meditation proceeds in the right way it will leave

behind a spiritual strength. One should not think that this strengthening has not occurred if one has not yet been able to feel it. We often reap the fruits years afterwards which we had not expected. One who with patience contents himself with little and does not demand soul-growth with greed and impatience will always receive an increase of spiritual strength. For every meditation sooner or later releases in us strengthening forces.

During meditation everything must be left outside that is connected with external life. The gateway through which we pass in meditation is like a narrow crevice. Every foreign thought that we take into meditation works like a destroying fire upon what should germinate within our inner being. The temptation to take such thoughts with us is immensely great.

Since through our meditation we are enabled to develop more quickly and thus help to further the evolution of humanity, meditation is just the field into which the hindering powers seek to enter and bring destroying influences by, for example, summoning everyday affairs into our memory. Now we have an occult remedy for protection against these unwanted thoughts and reducing them to silence. One should set before oneself as vividly as possible the Mercury Staff, a radiant staff round which there coils a black snake. Then one should imagine a shining snake that twines round in the opposite way. The black snake symbolizes the material thoughts which disturb us, as they are connected with our lower self, whereas the light snake represents the divine thoughts of the higher Self. If we set this symbol in its whole significance before our soul, seeing how the shining snake coils in the opposite way to the black one, then the disturbances will disappear and we can devote ourselves unhindered to our meditation.

It must be emphasized that it is not a question of advancing as rapidly as possible; many students think to attain progress by perpetually demanding new exercises. A student's strength of soul is shown just by the fact that he can continue with an exercise for a long time and draw strength from it – often throughout a whole lifetime. Every meditation formula is endowed with great power, lasting a long time in order to awaken the slumbering life-forces. The further a student advances and the more the spiritual forces awaken in him, so much the simpler the exercises which he receives.

Above all, the meditative life rests upon the fact of recapitulation. In this way the meditation becomes a continuous inner force, as when a drop falls perpetually on a stone and finally hollows it out. For the meditation to be present in our soul only once or ten times is not enough to bring about the densifying of this inner force. Only patience can bring it to such development that we become aware of our eternal germ of being. For this force is the essential thing and yet men often shun it. We can only take in the Powers of the spiritual world if we bring to them this inner stillness in the right way. They can only become aware of us if we come towards them through our life of imagination.

Enthusiasm of feeling must go parallel with selfless meditation, yet strengthening of thought must be there too. Certain mystics try to crush down thoughts completely and only foster the life of feeling.

Every esoteric student advances if he does his exercises faithfully and regularly, even if he is dissatisfied with his success. Above all things it is a matter of honest effort. Through meditating one actually becomes a different person; this comes about infallibly, whether one notices it or not.

It is necessary to repeat the exercises for a long time, sometimes for decades before the soul becomes inwardly sufficiently strengthened. For forces must be developed which are slumbering in the soul and which can be aroused when attentiveness and surrender are immeasurably enhanced. Through this activity the soul gradually achieves the experience of making itself, as a being of soul and spirit, free from the physical body and independent. And in the course of time one is able to unite a real meaning with the words: You experience yourself now as a being of spirit and soul; without being served by your senses and limbs, you experience yourself outside your body. One has reached a certain fruitful point in development when one sees one's own bodily nature from outside, just as one may have any other object of the physical world before one. As a rule one first succeeds in releasing the faculty of thought from the bodily instruments of brain and nervous system, so that one is aware of oneself in a free weaving of thinking, resting entirely on itself, outside the nervous system and the brain.

The first practical experience gives one the consciousness of living in thought as if in the environment of the head. One knows that one lives and weaves without employing the instrument of the brain and that this weaving in thought is accomplished outside the head. One particular impression remains unforgettable if it has once been experienced, namely, that on dipping down again into the nervous system and the brain these both offer a material resistance, so that a certain force is required for re-entering the body after one has experienced oneself for a time outside it.

The thinking activity of the soul is the first to be set free from the body, not as yet the activities of feeling and willing. Yet for true spiritual investigation these must also become independent and an infinite enhancement of surrender can alone bring it about. We may get an idea of this enhanced faculty of surrender if we use the comparison of sleep, where man's soul, separated from the body in its complete immobility, is given up to the common course of the universe. We mix nothing of our conscious thinking, feeling and willing in this sleep-condition. Through our meditation we must call forth this natural condition arbitrarily, with the difference that here the enhanced power of surrender leads to a heightened state of consciousness. The spiritual investigator must bring about the silence of all the senses, just as in sleep attention is turned away from every impression of the outer world. But whereas in sleep the soul sinks into unconsciousness through the faculty of spiritual surrender, it awakens in the divine spiritual stream of the cosmic forces to a consciousness compared with which the everyday consciousness seems but a state of sleep.

Through such activities of the soul and a complete cessation of the life of ideas bound to the brain and of the entire speech organism, the spiritual investigator is gradually able to develop inwardly the same force as is otherwise manifested outwardly through the body.

In the night the pupils are to be found with their Masters on the astral plane. One who has established a bond with his Master through his meditation is drawn towards the Master through this union. This is an event taking place during the night.

Every individual who carries out the necessary meditations can participate in such intercourse and come thereby to his higher Self. That which in some thousands of years will be our highest Self now rests in the bosom of the Masters. In order therefore to make actual acquaintance with our higher Self, we must seek it where it is to be found today — with the Higher Individualities. That is the intercourse of the pupil with the Master through meditation.

All spatial concepts, which only exist on the physical plane, must be eliminated during the meditation; nevertheless colour, light, sound, scent connected with sense impressions are also present in the astral world. For this reason it is good to form concepts as full as possible of content, since spiritual beings are expressing themselves in all that is perceived by the senses. They ray out their spiritual essence in colours, tones, scents. Thus, with the word 'light' one should represent to oneself a brilliance, filled with light, experiencing how the light-filled rays flow down to us.

While in this way one immerses oneself in certain ideas and eternal thoughts, one creates in one's etheric body life-preserving, organ-forming impressions. Similarly we can also meditate on the concept *Weisheit* (wisdom), yet not in firmly outlined definitions but by awakening in us mobile ideas and perceptions of it. If one meditates in the right way on the concept wisdom, something of wisdom itself will flow down upon us and grant us illumination out of the higher worlds.

In earlier ages intercourse with the divine spiritual worlds could only be brought about through the use of mantras and sound. Today, through words filled with meaning and content, man can prepare the way in his inner being for the union with the Christ-force. When the pupil succeeds in entirely shutting himself off in his meditation from external influences and noise, when he is able to eliminate the physical body, he is then living only in the etheric body, astral body and ego. Something like a magnetic fluid must draw us across into the spiritual worlds in our meditation; then we are on the right path. It is not the words themselves that matter, but that the right meaning and content should stream into us as a life-awakening force from the spiritual worlds, that they should be filled with meaning through the Christ-force. The words of the meditation formulae are chosen in such a way that they work quite impersonally; they are a garment in which the Logos streaming through the world can clothe Itself. The words must be in keeping with these flowing currents of the Logos and they are therefore chosen and arranged very definitely.

It is possible so to regard the esoteric life that one looks on the exercises which one receives as an adjunct to one's ordinary life. One would find then, however, that the progress made was not very considerable. The aim of the esoteric pupil should far rather consist in resolving to bring into connection with his esoteric life all that meets him in everyday existence. In this way he creates a centre in himself from which he directs the whole conduct of his life.

Through our meditation we should develop a strong force which uses the meditation-words as instruments for gradually moulding the spiritual organs in our astral body. It is by means of these organs that we can perceive the spiritual environment. The impressions that we imprint in our astral body will only become permanent in the course of time, for the astral body may be likened to an elastic mass that may assuredly receive an impression but after a time reverts to its former shape. These impressions are stamped into the astral body during sleep, when together with the ego it has deserted the physical body. The stronger and more intensive our meditation the more strongly are these impressions engraved into the astral body, until they ultimately become permanent and the soul's organs can develop from them.

If one makes oneself blind and deaf to all outer sense-impressions during the meditation, one slowly raises one's etheric body out of the physical body and unites with the Christ-aura which is now the aura of our earth. Were we to rise out of the body without the content of our meditation, our soul would be alone by itself. Now, however, it is permeated by the Christ and experiences the words of Paul: 'Yet not I live, but Christ liveth in me!'

The act of meditating represents a middle state by which the one-sided luciferic and ahrimanic elements may be overcome. Luciferic enticement lies in solitary thinking and brooding. The ahrimanic temptation lies in perception one-sidedly directed towards the external world. Now a middle condition can be developed in one's soul by making one's thoughts inwardly so strong and active that they come before one like something living, something to be heard and seen. This is a middle condition which is attained through meditation. Meditating is neither thinking nor perceiving; it is a thinking that lives as actively in the soul as a perception, and it is a perception that is directed not to an external object but to thoughts. Between the luciferic element of thought and the ahrimanic element of perception the soul-life in meditation flows into a divinely spiritual middle state that only bears within it the advancement of world evolution.

The man whose thoughts have become living forces in him through his meditation is living in the divine stream. On the right he has mere thoughts, on the left mere perception, and he excludes neither the one nor the other; he knows that polarities must keep each other in balance, just as a triangle is determined by the sum of its angles.

Meditation denotes the surrender to thoughts and feelings which are specially suited to our individuality and with which we completely identify ourselves. It is natural for human efforts easily to grow weak upon this path, for it means overcoming again and again if one is to reach this inner silencing of the soul. But in time one gets the feeling: Up to the present I have always merely thought this thought; now it begins to unfold a life, an inner activity of its own. It is as if one had actually brought forth a being out of oneself. The thought begins to take on an inner structure. It is an important moment when one realizes that the thought is only a covering for a definite living spiritual entity. One can therefore say to oneself: Your efforts have brought you to the point of providing a stage upon which something may develop that you have now awakened to its own existence. This coming alive of the meditative thought is a significant moment. Then the pupil notes that he is laid hold of by the objectivity of the spirit; he knows that the spiritual world concerns itself with him, as it were, that it has come near to him.

Something of the utmost importance takes place in self-less meditation; through this intimate process of meditating, a fine consumption of warmth is produced. Every

meditation is linked with a delicate warmth and light process. Warmth and light are used up by us when we meditate
and this gives rise to a life-process. In our ordinary thinking
a warmth process also takes place in our organism and this
brings about memory. It must not come to this, however,
during meditation. If we live in the pure thought-content,
then what we consume inwardly of warmth and light is not
impressed into our body but into the general cosmic ether.
And this causes an external process in our surroundings.
During a genuine meditation we impress the form of our
thought upon the universal ether: and if in our retrospection we observe a meditation process, we are not confronted with a memory but with an objective perception of
the imprints in the cosmic ether.

One who engages in true meditation is living in a process
which is at the same time a world process. What takes place
is the following. In meditating, warmth is consumed and
therefore cold ensues; the universal ether is cooled down.
And since light, too, is consumed, it is dimmed down,
darkness ensues. It is always possible to a clairvoyant to tell
if a person has meditated somewhere; a shadow-image of
him remains behind which is actually cooler than the surroundings. Something has been effected which one can
compare with the print on a photographic plate.

If we reflect upon this we shall be able to understand how
someone returning to earth in his following earthly life still
finds the traces of his meditation thoughts in the cosmic
ether. Here we have a concrete example of the working of
karma. The meditator comes more and more to the feeling:
It is not merely you, with your thoughts; something tran-
spires into which no doubt you are placed, but it goes on
outside you as something that remains. This 'feeling of
oneself as in the atmosphere of the weaving and being of
one's thoughts', as if thoughts move through us like waves,
gives us a definite feeling. It is the assured feeling that one
stands in a spiritual world and is oneself but a weaving

member in the general weaving of the divine world. And it is a remarkable feeling that then comes over us in the stillness of our soul: it is not you alone that creates that—it is created! You have begun to stir these waves but they spread themselves out around you. They have a life of their own of which you are but the centre.

That is an experience which unlocks for us the knowledge of the spiritual world. It is an experience of extraordinary significance to which, however, patience, endurance, resignation, belong. This experience serves to give complete conviction of the presence of the spiritual world.

The most important, significant moments for our development in our esoteric life are those *after* the meditation, when we let absolute calm enter our soul in order to allow the content of the meditation to work upon it. We must strive to extend these moments more and more, for through this 'lifting ourselves' out of the circle of our everyday thoughts and feelings, through the 'emptying itself' of our soul, we unite with a world from which pictures come towards us, pictures that we can compare with nothing out of our usual life.

If after every meditation we awaken in ourselves a feeling of gratitude and awe—a feeling that one can call a mood of prayer—and are conscious at the same time of the grace in which we have participated, we shall realize that we are on the right path and that the spiritual worlds come towards us.

The Retrospect

In the evening, before going to sleep, we should prepare ourselves to enter the spiritual worlds, yet not by egotistic petitions for happiness and so on, but by a mood of gratitude that we shall again be taken into the bosom of the Spiritual Beings. Here the practice of retrospection plays a great role. The past day is to come again before us in picture form, yet in the reverse order of its events, that is, in a backward direction. And with each experience that we had in the day we must ask ourselves: Did I do that right, could I not have done it still better? It is very important to learn to look on ourselves as a stranger, as if we observed and criticized ourselves from outside. We must try to get as clear a picture as possible of the day's events. It is far more important to be able to remember little details than striking events. A general who has fought a great battle will have the whole picture of the fight before his eyes in the evening; this is impressed upon his mind, yet he will no longer be aware of how he put on his boots or took them off. We must get as complete a picture as possible. We see ourselves, for instance, cross the street. Try to remember how the rows of houses went, what shop windows we passed, what people met us, how they looked, how we ourselves looked. Then we see ourselves enter a shop and remember which assistant came forward, what she wore, how she spoke, etc. These details require a great effort, but that is just what strengthens the forces of the soul. There is no need to think it will take an hour. At first one will remember very little. Finally, however, the whole course of the day will pass in five minutes through the soul like moving pictures, clear in every detail.

Nevertheless one must strive for it with patience; one who merely lets the day's events pass before him superficially gains no benefit from this exercise. Its purpose is the following. If a man has walked some distance, and at the end of the road would like to recognize the portion he has covered, he can do this in two ways. He can stand with his back to the road and try to remember what lies behind him, or he can turn round and actually look at it. After passing through a period of time we can at first only *remember* it in our memory, not as yet actually *look* back on it. But the retrospect which we only apply to space can also be applied to time. In this way we learn to read the Akasha Chronicle in which every event is inscribed. At first one can only recognize in it things concerning oneself. Later one learns to read other things too.

This is also connected with the transforming of memory which disappears in its abstract form in an esoteric student and something else takes its place. We acquire the faculty of *seeing* the past directly, and no longer need the ordinary memory. The following is a good exercise. Before going to sleep read about seven lines from *Occult Science*, impressing the contents upon one's mind without learning it by heart, and then recall it the next morning. One soon acquires a certain skill, with practice, that benefits and strengthens the memory. This retrospection is the means by which spiritual pictures are created and taken over with us into the spiritual world. That it must be taken in the backward direction is connected with the passage of time in the spiritual world which moves in a direction opposite to the order in the physical world. By our usual thinking forwards we set ourselves, as it were, against the spiritual worlds and repulse them. Many students lament that they go to sleep in the evening meditation, but this fact too can mean an advance. One should of course take pains to stay awake, yet it need not always be a failure to go to sleep. For it would appear that the exercise is continued after falling asleep. If one wakes in the night one should try to remember the exercise at the very place where it was broken off. One can then have the feeling that it had meanwhile gone on working in one. If this is so we should try to remember what has worked on in us unconsciously in the interval. This can gradually bring about a conscious entry into the spiritual world.

Before one begins a meditation one should make sure that there is time to carry it through to the end. It is not well to break it off, because Ahriman can then make it his own possession. And going through it without full thought will also give him this opportunity. Sooner or later we shall learn through our meditation to know the spiritual worlds, but we must always take care that this comes about with the right intention. It must not be out of curiosity, but in order to help humanity. To take nothing relating to sympathies and antipathies and our petty cares over into the spiritual world will open it for us in the right way and let us enter. Even merely fulfilling the customary moral code, however conscientiously, is not enough for the esoteric student. For here egotism can easily enter and someone may for instance say to himself: I will be good so that people will think me good. The esoteric pupil does not do right in order to be considered good, but because he gradually recognizes that good alone brings the evolution of the world forward, while evil and the thoughtless and base put hindrances in the path of evolution. All meditation and concentration and other exercises become worthless, in fact in a certain sense even harmful, if a person's life is not in keeping with these conditions.

One cannot provide a man with forces, one can only bring to development those already lying within him. Nor do they evolve of themselves, because there are outer and inner hindrances. The external hindrances are removed through definite rules of life, and the inner through the special instructions on meditation and concentration, etc. We can make what we think so inwardly alive, so full of power, that we have our own thoughts before us like a living thing that becomes as concrete to us as what we hear and see. That is a middle condition. In the mere thought that underlies brooding there lies the approach to man of Lucifer; in mere listening, whether through perception or through outer authority, lies the ahrimanic element. If one inwardly strengthens and awakens the soul so that one almost hears and sees one's thoughts, then this is true meditation. Going through our exercises with devotion and earnestness is the esoteric means for the loosening of our body. Through the withdrawal of the etheric body the physical body begins to resemble a plant from which the sap is for a time withdrawn. The plant dries up and so too, though one does not see it physically, the physical body partially dries, and where it has a tendency to illnesses these appear. But when the etheric body has rightly saturated itself with spiritual truths it draws new forces to itself and these work again in a healing way upon the physical body. We are to reach the point where the 'lotus flowers' unfold in the etheric body through the imprint of the astral body.

We should feel the words of the meditation to be as much as possible filled with colour, light and sound. We should feel them through and through, live right into them. Spiritual beings live in colours and tones and by uniting ourselves with definite sense perceptions, definite beings flow into us. Through esoteric work we should assimilate a new thinking, new feeling and new willing. We must let a thought that we have thought pass over into our feeling and fully permeate this with it. The fluctuating thinking that comes at the moment of waking is the cosmic thinking that lives in us. We can be in it if our dream is not merely experienced as a reflection, as most are, but as if we were actually in it, moved in our soul, present in our spirit. Concepts gained on the physical plane are of absolutely no assistance in penetrating into the spiritual worlds. All that we may retain is power of forming concepts, and sense of truth and logic — moreover, the faculty to form new concepts and the sense for the new truths that one will learn to know.

What is experienced inwardly in meditation and concentration acts on the astral body as the light on the physical eye, sound on the ear, for these were developed through light and sound. The astral body is reorganized through these inner experiences of meditation; the organs of knowledge for the higher worlds are drawn out of it just as were the physical sense organs through sound and light.

These organs, however, will only become permanent in the astral body if they are impressed, imprinted in the etheric or life-body. Now as long as the etheric body is within the physical body it is very difficult for the experiences of the astral body to impress themselves upon it. In former ages it was impossible for what had evolved in the astral body through meditation and concentration to be imprinted into the etheric body if this remained united with the physical body. When we consider that the sense-world actually only exists for us because the organs of the physical body have been chiselled out in it, it will not seem particularly astonishing to hear that such higher organs are also built into man's higher members, the etheric and astral bodies. Today man's physical body is organized, but not yet his higher bodies. The higher organs become formed in one who strives for initiation. And in order to form them the astral body must be taken where it exists in purity. The lifting out of the etheric body is by no means easy today.

Man will increasingly recognize the need for real thought-concentration in order to hold the entire soul life together in these thoughts. He must direct his whole soul life upon sharply outlined thoughts that he places before his consciousness, whereas he would otherwise let his senses stray from one thing to another, one fact to another. Thus he will more and more, even if for a short time only, direct the thought life upon definite things that he chooses for himself.

Through the vitalizing of the concepts of spiritual science one can resemble a man who sits in a train or on a ship and who must exert himself inwardly against the noises and rattle so as to hear nothing of it but be entirely enclosed in himself. One can only do this today with the concepts of spiritual science. But one must bear in mind that it requires continually renewed recapitulation, for it is this that gives the strength. Then one remains in oneself, by oneself, calm and assured. The powers of the spiritual world can enter if we meet them rightly with this composure. This alone can give us the consciousness that through such conceptual life as has been described we come towards these powers. The important thing is to feel that, independent of our reasoning life, something thinks in us of which we can say: Not I, but *it* thinks in me. Although such thoughts mean little to us at first, yet we can strengthen and further them through a feeling of gratitude to the Higher Powers. If we say after each such moment, however, short, 'I think you, ye Powers of the Higher Hierarchies, that you have let me perceive this,' then through the feeling of gratitude and awe these moments increase in which higher worlds will reveal themselves. We shall be able to hold in memory what at first moved through our soul dim as a dream and ultimately we shall be able to summon such conditions as well. Then we shall gradually become clear that this thinking in us is always independent of our intellectual thought.

Gratitude is the vessel that we lift to the Gods that they may fill it with their wonder-gifts. If in all earnestness we foster the feeling of thankfulness, then gratitude, loving devotion must be there to the invisible spiritual givers of life; and it is the most beautiful way to be led from one's personality to the supersensible if this guidance goes through gratitude. Gratitude ultimately brings us to veneration and love of the life-bestowing spirit of man. It gives birth to love and love makes the heart open for the spirit-powers pervading life. If after every meditation we arouse in ourselves the feeling of gratefulness and reverence — a feeling that we can call a mood of prayer — and be aware in what grace we are taking part, we shall realize that we are on the right path for the spiritual worlds to approach us.

We must form a different idea about the experiences that come to us at first. We complain, for instance, that thoughts storm into our meditation which trouble and disturb us. If we were to consider it more closely we should recognize that it is an advance, that we have become more sensitive since we perceive that these thoughts are stronger than ourselves. They oblige us to exercise more force in our meditation, for it is luciferic beings who are drawing up our own thoughts. These luciferic beings are always in us but they are submerged by the fluctuations of our everyday life. In the stillness we create in our meditation, we are able to notice what otherwise the stir of daily life conceals. The whole constitution and condition of our bodily nature changes when we meditate. However badly and incapably we meditate, we nevertheless draw the ego and astral body and a portion of the etheric out of our physical body, and hence in the moments after meditation we may have remarkable experiences in our etheric body. Inspirations from the higher worlds can also come to us for the material world. It is a matter of our efforts. Through these exercises we really become different beings, and this happens inevitably, even if we are not aware of it. For in all the exercises, whether they are given in books or verbally, there lie the forces which loosen the etheric body and lift it out of the physical body. It is another matter, however, to become aware of these alterations.

The soul may already possess organs—but there is a decided difference whether it sleeps or wakes, in its spiritual environment. In order to awake and become conscious, the soul needs strong forces and preparation. Many people make this becoming conscious more difficult because they always picture the spiritual world like a second physical world, only finer, more penetrable. That is a great hindrance, for then we do not observe the delicate symptoms of awakening. He who assimilates esoteric explanations rightly, can, however, *conceive* how the spiritual world is experienced when the soul awakes. In order to succeed in this one must first ask oneself: What is the actual nature of thinking? It is supersensible; one is always in the supersensible world with human thinking. We live in the thinking but we have no direct experience of it. What we experience in it are its mirrorings on the physical body. The brain is the mirror. Now, through esoteric training one should come to an experience of the thinking itself, not merely of the thoughts. It is a great step to this experience. And a further one follows, that is, man feels all that is good, right, true in his thinking stream out of him. He feels it as a growing into the future, as forming the seed for his future. But the false, wrong, unlovely things that he thinks and feels also grow out in the same way. He feels them outstreaming quite concretely and he knows that the bad thoughts streaming from him will serve as nourishment to the good in the future. He therefore learns to understand why so many distorted, unlovely thoughts and feelings beset him in meditation. The evil powers like people who make progress through meditation better than the ordinary person, and fasten upon them all the more strongly in order to do them harm. If one sets before one's soul the black wooden cross with the seven roses, the evil powers must give way and yield.

Thoughts in meditation should be formed clearly, sharply, distinctly, a purely spiritual act taking its course in full self-possession. The physical and etheric organism must remain completely undisturbed during meditation. With correct meditation one comes to the point of living with the developed content of thought forces outside one's physical and etheric organism. One looks at it and it radiates back in thought-forms what one experiences in the ether. One has the etheric experience in one's own organism, one has attained personal experience in the relationship of a relative objectivity.

One must meditate in pictures if one would actually enter one's inner being. Hence the effect of ceremonial, filling one with real enthusiasm; all of a ritual nature has this effect, not only external ceremonial but the understanding *of the world in pictures*. As long as one tries to come to inner self-knowledge through abstract ideas and concepts, no effect is produced. As soon as one submerges into one's inner being with pictures that illuminate the soul's experiences, one grasps oneself inwardly.

In the course of higher development the pupil, though only for a short time in the day, forsakes the lower self of his ordinary life through which he confronts the outer world. During meditation he leaves it to itself; he takes away its guardian, as it were, who is otherwise in continuous control, who regulates the peculiarities of character, perhaps repressing them or at least keeping them in check. Now since this lower ego is left to itself, though only for a short time, there creep from all sides out of hidden corners of our nature, qualities that we thought we had already overcome, the repression of which had seemed to us quite easy. In a certain way a man can thus become worse, unless he continually exercises the strictest control over himself. But we should also be grateful to the Gods for our faults, since battling with them makes us strong and free. Not for a moment, however, should we on this account approve of them. If we struggle and strive earnestly and incessantly we shall feel that the faulty element in us dies away.

No deterioration, however, is possible if the student pays enough heed to himself and to his life and surroundings. Above all, the esotericist should keep before him in his daily meditation that his whole aim is to reach his higher Self, and he should ponder over its nature. He must not think that he is to bring something towards it, but should maintain an attitude of expectation, as if awaiting all from it. The higher Self must draw us in our meditation over into the spiritual worlds like a magnetic fluid. Then we are in the right frame of mind. Yet it is not so much a question of words (the words are only to furnish the garment) but that the right import should stream from them into us out of the spiritual world, that our thought is filled with the power of the Christ — that is what matters.

Publisher's Note Regarding
Rudolf Steiner's Lectures

The lectures contained in this volume have been translated from the German which is based on stenographic and other recorded texts that were in most cases never seen or revised by the lecturer. Hence, due to human errors in hearing and transcription, they may contain mistakes and faulty passages. Every effort has been made to ensure that this is not the case. Some of the lectures were given to audiences more familiar with anthroposophy; these are the so-called 'private' or 'members' lectures. Other lectures, like the written works, were intended for the general public. The differences between these, as Rudolf Steiner indicates in his autobiography *The Course of My Life*, is twofold. On the one hand, the members' lectures take for granted a background in and commitment to anthroposophy; in the public lectures this was not the case. At the same time, the members' lectures address the concerns and dilemmas of the members, while the public work speaks directly out of Steiner's own understanding of universal needs. Nevertheless, as Rudolf Steiner stresses: 'Nothing was ever said that was not solely the result of my direct experience of the growing content of anthroposophy. There was never any question of concessions to the prejudices and preferences of the members. Whoever reads these privately printed lectures can take them to represent anthroposophy in the fullest sense. Thus it was possible without hesitation—when the complaints in this direction became too persistent—to depart from the custom of circulating this material "for members only". But it must be borne in mind that faulty passages do occur in these reports not revised by myself.' Earlier in the same chapter, he states: 'Had I been able to correct them [the private lectures] the restriction [for members only] would have been unnecessary from the beginning.'

Rudolf Steiner
SELF-TRANSFORMATION

At the heart of Rudolf Steiner's spiritual philosophy is the esoteric path of inner development that can lead to true self-transformation. In these lectures, Steiner shows how — by developing certain qualities such as clear thinking, inner tranquillity and positivity, as well as through meditative exercises — it is possible to break out of the shadowy, brain-bound world of everyday consciousness. The first step on this path of transformation is the level of Imagination, where the spiritual world is seen in pictures. Steiner indicates how one can then attain to the levels of Inspiration, and finally to the highest stage of Intuition.

As a highly-trained clairvoyant, Rudolf Steiner speaks on this question from his own spiritual experience. In contrast to many of the New Age paths available today, however, his methods are based on the western tradition, the Rosicrucian path of initiation, as opposed to older Eastern teachings. This modern path is, he suggests, a metamorphosis of the Eastern paths, and is best suited to modern consciousness.

RUDOLF STEINER PRESS
256 pages; ISBN 1 85584 019 7; £11.95